27 SHADES OF GREEN

THE TRUE COLORS OF AN AMERICAN SMALL FARMER

GARY ROMANO

If America could be once again, a nation of self-reliant farmers, craftsman, hunters, ranchers and artists, then the rich would have little power to dominate others. Neither to serve nor to rule. That was the American dream.

Edward Abbey

Table of Contents

Introduction

The winters are harsh, most times below zero, for periods of time. Permafrost is inevitable as it hardens the landscape. Winter time is cold and blustery in Sierra Valley as I look out over the farm on an early January day across this vast 130 square mile alpine valley, the ground covered in white frost and partial snow, with a bone-chilling east wind, as I look at the thermometer of nine degrees. All vegetation is in skeleton form and looking lifeless, I think about what my uncles told me growing up on this vivacious dairy and cattle ranch, "Why all you have in Sierra Valley is July and winter...most times you can't grow a weed." I put on my insulated coveralls, down vest and jacket, secure my "beanie" cap over my ears, and put on my wool gloves and bolt out the door into this outdoor freezer...I say "Come on Chloe, let's go check out the well houses and the greenhouses ", Chloe is my English black lab, with tail-a-wagging, she bolts ahead of me grabbing a stick off the ground and goes prancing through what little snow she can find, oblivious to the cold, she's just happy to go for our routine walk. It's our routine morning and afternoon walk to check out the farm and make sure I don't have any frozen pipes or problems that can happen overnight. We walk down my driveway, an old abandoned county road that was given to my family in the fifties by the road department when they built the new Plumas County Road A-23 here in Beckwourth, California. The driveway is long, about a quarter mile, fractured with the evidence of 80 years of wear and tear, freeze and thaw that leaves a resemblance of the past, Chloe and I walk to the end of the southern entrance then turn around and walk back to the north entrance checking that the light bulbs and heat tape are working in our two well houses and inspecting my four hoop houses for vole damage and the conditions of my winter greens. Along our walk, I can't help look at the vast Sierra Valley, the largest alpine valley in the western hemisphere, one hour north of Lake Tahoe at 5000 feet elevation. All the vegetation has a dull green tint to them holding on to a sliver of life during these hard winters. The mountain perennial grasses, mostly bunch grasses are mostly brown, with a touch of green at its base reminding me that they are hibernating until spring, the sage brush and bitterbrush are a dull green-grayish with brown tips that were the fall flower stalks, and the mountains around Sierra Valley are full of evergreen ponderosa pine, incense cedar and white fir.

When I bought the farm from my uncles in 1989, I was the only family member that was interested in buying the last family ranch, an old abandoned dairy/cattle ranch. My Aunt Betty and Uncle Emilio were getting up in age and they didn't want to take care of the last 65 acre ranch, it was too much for them and their kids had careers and family in the Bay Area. On my first walk, similar to what I do today, I noticed a common theme on the ranch, because of our cool climate and temperatures during each of our seasons: Spring, summer, fall and winter there were very few different colors in the landscape other than green. All the pasture grasses were different shades of green, most of the shrubs (sagebrush, rabbit brush, bitterbrush, buckbrush, serviceberry, chokecherry)were shades of green, and the trees were evergreen of pines, fir, and cedar…yes there was short periods of spring wildflowers, and shrubs with inconspicuous flowers blooming but most of the year were shades of green.

I coined the title of this book; *Twenty Seven Shades of Green* actually about fifteen years ago when I started experimenting with growing vegetables. I soon realized that here in Sierra Valley, Plumas County, Beckwourth, California, all I could grow were winter vegetables during the summer months because our summer temperatures were equivalent to the rest of California's winter temperatures which were 30-40 degrees in the morning and 70-85 degrees in the afternoons. As I looked at my five acres of vegetables, yes they were all shades of green: salad greens, chard greens, arugula greens, kale greens, mustard greens, mizuna greens, spinach greens, romaine greens....Greens, Greens, Greens....of all shades, speckled in were mixed colors of greens like carrots, radishes, beets, turnips, green onions, broccoli, broccoli raab, rapini, and cabbage...thus the title: TWENTY-SEVEN SHADES OF GREEN!

This book is actually my fifth publication dealing with plants and farming. I've always been intrigued with native plants, the natural landscape and the farming lifestyle, even though I ran from farming as I reached college, then my roots (being raised in a farming/ranching family) pulled me back to farming when I bought this ranch, and I'm still farming after all these years! At Cal Poly San Luis Obispo, Ca. I first self-published WILD EDIBLE PLANTS OF SAN LUIS OBISPO COUNTY in 1982; Then for my Master's Degree at Chico State University, Chico Ca. I finished my thesis project on TREKKING FOR WILD EDIBLE PLANTS IN SOUTHERN CALIFORNIA, that never got published in 1986; onto the wonderful Bona Fide Books with Kim Wyatt I have WHY I FARM: Risking it All for a Life on the Land in 2013; JULY AND WINTER: Growing Food in the Sierra in 2016; and now TWENTY-SEVEN SHADES OF GREEN: The True Colors of a Small Organic Farmer.

The first two books were native plant books, and Why I Farm is a wonderful read of family memoirs and a call to action for consumers and farmers that we need more small farms and farmers. July & Winter is a "how-to" book, reference book if you will, on how to grow food in the Sierra indoors and out, a one of its kind anywhere in the West.

What I hope to do with TWENTY-SEVEN SHADES OF GREEN is to combine nature, the amazing shades of green, memoirs, and farmer wisdom within each chapter and over the course of the book, highlighting my 61 years as a third generation farmer into a fun read, and leaving you with some insight on how I see the future of farming, our food systems, and the challenges that our law makers and politicians have set forth for the small American farmer. This book is to bring awareness to the reader that we are losing small farmers at an alarming rate and I hope to inspire new farmers that we need them badly to replace us aging farmers. In addition, consumers must understand that if we don't promote our local farmers, farmers markets and support our local food coop's we are going to only be buying fruits and vegetables from other countries. Throughout the book my shades of green will appear in chapters as to how they have influenced my life and most small farmers. It is my hope that you continue to support small sustainable farms and the organic food movement to improve the health of our communities and America.

After I decided on the title, it became more evident to me that the color green does typify most farms, farmers, and the natural landscape, especially in my lifetime of farming. Each chapter will be a shade of green that typifies that chapter. There is no other color that represents a farmer better than Green, especially this mountain organic farmer! Sustainability is all about being Green! It is the sanctuary away from stresses of modern living *(the green room)* restoring us back to a sense of well-being. Green is an emotional positive color, allowing us the ability to love and nurture ourselves and others like the "family unit", the family farm. A natural peacemaker, it must avoid to become a martyr (Dark Green). Green is the observer, the social worker, charity worker loving to contribute to society (a farmer producing food for the community).

Green promotes a love of nature, "going green", and a love of family, friends, pets and the home (farm). It is the color of the garden/nature lover, home/farm lover and the good host. Of course green is the national color of Ireland, the shamrock (green) is associated with good luck, leprechauns, clovers, and St. Patrick's Day. Green relates to stability and endurance, giving us persistence and strength to cope with adversity. It is the color of prosperity and wealth "*the green stuff* "of money, in the business world. On the negative, dark green can be possessive and materialistic (as in corporate greed), and dark being selfish, miserable, devious with money and inconsiderate, or over cautious and a power monger (military green/camo).

What's great about the shades of green is the color green represents the good and the bad. I think that's why so many cartoon characters are in the color green. There are actually twenty seven shades of green cartoon figures: *Kermit the Frog; Creatures of the Black Lagoon; the Green-Eyed Monster; the Grinch; Slimer; Frankenstein; Gumby; Teenage Mutant Ninja Turtles; Swamp Thing; The Hulk; Jolly Green Giant; Green Hornet; Yoda; Gremlins; Wicked Witch of the West; Mad Hatter; Godzilla; Shrek; Beast Boy; She-Hulk; Green Goblin; Plankton; Gamora; Green Lantern; Iron Fist; Green Arrow; and Poison Ivy...* twenty seven shades of green cartoon characters. The title of one of my last chapters is Dark Green, depicts the darker future of farming. To lighten up the chapter of Dark Green I've assigned cartoon names to the "villains" in agriculture and also assigned cartoon names to the superheroes in agriculture to have a little fun with such a heavy subject, titling the Chapter, *Farming into the Abyss.*

More than ever before we have to "think green" to reverse the direction of Trump Administration who has deteriorated environmental laws to allow off-shore oil drilling; threaten to remove The Clean Water Act; has removed the Farmers Fair Market Practices Act; removed the animal welfare standards for factory farms; remove bans on toxic pesticides; watered down the NOP (National Organic Program) standards to allow aquaponics and hydroponics to be considered organic, to name a few. I will elaborate in my chapter Farming into the Abyss, about the unknown future, and the ominous challenges that the small farms face in the coming years in America. Stay tuned!

Here are some facts for you to think about while you're enjoying my farming journey on this roller coaster ride through life and through it all I'm still farming after all these years!

An American farm is defined by the USDA as any operation that contributes a minimum of $1000 per year of agricultural product to the economy, plant or animal. Some facts to consider:

- As of 2014, only 1 percent of all occupations in the US are farmers.
- Farms with Ag sales of $25,000 or less account for 67 percent of the farms and only two percent of the total Ag sales.
- Farms with Ag sales over one million dollars account for 66 percent of the total Ag sales and everyone else is in between.
- Farms over $250,000 equal 12 percent of the farms that are responsible for 89 percent of the food production in America.
- In 2012 the percentage of farmers turning a profit continued to decline since 2002. A farm grossing $100,000 to $250,000 had reduced its profit from $30,000 down to $26,000, and that's not enough for a family to live on.
- Currently 80 percent of farmers take off-farm jobs to supplement their income and 53 percent of farm couples are both working off the farm.
- Women constitute 30 percent of all farmers with 15 percent being the prime operators. Most of these women farmers are small farms with 91 percent of the farms with less than $50,000 in sales.
- Over the past 30 years, the USDA has reported the average age of farmers to be increasing steadily. From 2007-2012 it rose two percent to 58.3 years old (and as of 2018 it is my age at 61!)

Clearly you can see that a small amount of large farms are responsible for a large amount of the US food production and were losing more small farms every day. The future is looking dim and we must help the"Farmasaur!"

The data suggests that due to a rapid increase in start-up cost, and the increased value of purchasing land makes it prohibitive for young people to become farmers. This could lead to a serious skill gap when the older farmers retire…if they can.

So, we need another Green Revolution! Green Revolution is a term referring to a dramatic increase in agricultural productivity that occurred from 1950-1970. The Green Revolution originated as a geopolitical manifesto to develop plant varieties that would assist Third World countries in achieving agricultural self-sufficiency. Thus broadening the term to mean any significant increase in agriculture as a result of a scientific approach. The beginning of the GMO industry and seed and gene patents. Creating Industrial Agriculture and Factory Farms…"*Get Big or Get Out*" Secretary of the Interior Earl Butts said at the national farming conference under President Reagan, and big they became, full speed ahead! Livestock followed a similar pattern with artificial insemination to greatly enhance the advantages of selective breeding to create factory farms of poultry, swine, cattle, and dairy. So I can go on-and-on in this subject but another time another space.

To all of us, now is our time to renew our Green Revolution and "*think green*" again," *go small or not at all*"I say. Support your local farms and support farmers markets and CSA's (Community Supported Agriculture), create community and school gardens. Help create sustainable communities by reducing food wastes, recycling, removing plastic bags, water conservation, encourage renewable energy with wind, water and solar and remove exotic plant species and plant native plants, install erosion control and reforestation measures to protect our waterways .

The grower of Trees, the gardener, the man born to farming, who's hands reach into the ground and sprout, to him the soil is a devine drug. He enters into death yearly, and comes back rejoicing. He has seen the light lie down in the dung heap, and rise again in the corn.
—Wendell Berry

Sierra Valley Farms

Lime Green

Flower Fields Forever

"No water, No life. No blue, No green."

Sylvia Earle

Lime green: inspires youthfulness, playfulness, naivety, liked by most young people early in their lives. Lime green typifies spring: a time of tender new growth coming out of winter, to restore life and creates a feeling of anticipation.

Lime green represents the young farmers whose vitality and high energy to begin their new family farm. Most times with more energy than money, they jump into their new farming venture, naive, and full of "spit and vinegar" ...balls to the wall...full speed ahead with dreams and aspirations of growing organic food for their local communities and excited about their new lifestyle of not punching a clock or sitting at a desk in front of a computer screen, nine to five. They are their own bosses, living a healthy, free life and working long hours because it's their labor of love. It's the memoirs of my youth with my twin brother on mom and dad's flower farm of being vibrant and free, working hard and playing hard.

It's been a cold, and raining all day at Mom and Dad's flower farm in Morgan Hill, California, on a typical February Saturday in 1971. My twin brother Larry and I (14 years old) were cutting pussy willow for Dad to sell on Monday at the San Francisco Flower Market. We were in our weekend attire, irrigation rubber boots, and full raingear. It seemed to always be raining every weekend that we would help Mom and Dad at the farm during the winter months. We lived in Redwood City and it was the halfway point between the flower farm and the Flower Market in San Francisco. On this day, like so many between January and February, we would harvest (hand cut) the hedgerows of French-double pussy willow and to meet the orders Dad had for Mondays flower market and also for the upcoming week's markets, so Mom and Dad wouldn't have to cut so much during the week, you know…free labor.

The eight to ten foot high hedgerows of pussy willow bordered the twenty one acres of the farm and it seemed like the rows never ended. With hand-clippers in hand, stretched high over our heads, with the rain running down our sleeves and blinding our vision we would "snip, snip, cut, cut" each willow stem and when we had a handful create piles of about 200 stems placed on the ground, that Dad would then bale up with rope, and then we would then pick up the bales of willow and load them on our old "Green Acres"(as we called it because we hand painted it olive green, and I still have it on my farm today) 1949 Allis Chalmers wheel tractor with a small trailer and take them to the green metal-Quonset buildings to store. . ALL DAY LONG…from 9 am until 4pm Saturday and Sunday every weekend from January through February. It was hard work, slopping through the mud carrying these 50 pound bales of pussy willow to the trailer. Then during the week after school we would help dad cut and bunch the willow for the flower market. Work, work, work!

At its end in February the pussy willow was done (thank God!) and on came spring our season for cutting flowering quince, peach and cherry blossoms, lilacs and forsythia (woopie…but we weren't out of the woods yet) which we harvested the same way. The only difference was these limbs and stems of the blossoms were put into five gallon buckets of water to keep fresh for market. About fifteen acres in all, orchards of shrubs and tree blossoms were cover cropped in fields of yellow mustards in full bloom three feet tall with an understory of chickweed, filaree, and miner's lettuce, and yes all lime green in color symbolizing the youthful and playful spirit that Larry and I had on the farm in our youth, the realization that winter is over and summer is on the way! Plus we didn't have a choice; we did what had to be done to help the family. We worked as a family unit like spokes in a wheel.

The Romano flower business all began when my Grandpa Romano came over from Italy in 1915 to join his brother who had come out a couple years before and worked for a florist in San Francisco. My Grandpa, Giovanni Lodovico Romano (Nonno as we called him in Italian) then bought three acres in Redwood City in 1921 thus starting G. L. Romano Wholesale Florist. Dad was born in 1926 and it became G.L. Romano & Son Wholesale Florist until Mom and Dad retired in 2007. In that span Dad and Nonno began outgrowing the three acres in Redwood City by the 1940's and after WWII Dad and Nonno bought ten acres in Cupertino in 1948. Soon after Dad married Mom in 1956 and they build our home in Redwood City and in 1957 had two beautiful twin boys me and my brother Larry. The workforce was in place!! In 1958 we were taken over by eminent domain by Santa Clara County to build the Cupertino High School. Off we went looking for a new farm, continuing south to San Jose, Dad and Nonno found twelve acres along the Coyote Creek the farm that I remember most in my early youth. Larry and I loved that farm, surround by the active Coyote Creek which we spent hours playing in after work throughout the summer. In the summer months Dad and Mom planted acres and acres of flowers, and as a child and through my teens seemed like "flower fields forever", especially planting them, weeding on our hands and knees for hours, flood irrigating and moving miles and miles of hand-line irrigation pipes from the flower fields to the flowering shrub and tree orchards, not to mention hours and hours in the hot sun picking and bunching thousands of bunches of coxcomb, celosia, globe amaranth, asters and sunflowers.

Well lightning does strike twice. In 1970 our favorite county, Santa Clara County pulled another quick eminent domain on us saying that they needed our twelve acres to complete the Hellyer Park Bike Trail. Once again south we went where we ended up with our last farm a twenty one acre walnut and prune orchard in Morgan Hill, in which we had to remove all the trees and start over. They paid us for the loss of crops, but Larry and I never liked this farm as much because it didn't have any fun amenities like the Coyote Creek.

Throughout the years on all the farms we owned, moving from one to the next, we never had a real home on these farms, we lived in the residential area of Redwood City and that was our hub, but we spent the weekends at the farm in crazy make-shift housing arrangements. At the Coyote Creek farm sleeping amongst the tractors in a lime green steel garage with a table and hot plate, bottled water, with a pit toilet outside, that we were afraid to use as kids…Larry and I would just "hold it" until morning so we could just go out and find a secret spot and go! The Morgan Hill farm wasn't much better although we did have plumbed toilets and running water with a shower, but it was in these old migrant green metal "Labor houses" that were all bolted together with no insulation. It got too hot in the summer to stay inside and even colder during the winter to sleep in them. All we had was an old "pot-belly" stove to warm up the one room shack. Of course we hand painted them lime green…dad must have had a shit load of "Lime Green" paint. Everything got painted all different shades of green; green, tractors, buildings, furniture and equipment…all with a paint brush. Green was the color of choice, no matter what the object was…we sure had plenty of it! I think back now, I'm sure it was all lead-based paint, no wonder I'm crazy enough to keep farming after all these years!

Agriculture at that time was booming. The small farmers were in the "lime green" of their life! Small farms were very prosperous and bountiful in the Bay Area and along the peninsula coast. Especially the flower business, during the 1970's, and until the late 1980's, we grew fields and fields of flowers all year long. It was a lot of work for a family of four and especially during my late teens in high school and going to San Mateo Junior College I was thinking about girls and partying and didn't want to waste my weekends on the farm! Well in an Italian family work and family come first...in that order, but once the work was done it was party time! Dad would say "I don't care when you come in tonight but you have to be ready to go to the flower market by 2 am." Perfect, that's just when the bars close, I get my last call in around one and meet dad at the truck by two, and I did many times! Once we got to market and unloaded the flowers he would stick me in the back wrapping the flower bunches in newspaper, out of public contact, and delivering them to the florist trucks in the back allies, I guess he figured that I'd fit in with all the drunks I encountered along the way at that hour of the morning. But the flower market was fun! Well it was fun once you got there! It was crazy hours, Dad went to the market on Monday, Wednesday and Friday from 2 am and he sold out by 8am and had breakfast and heading home by 9am. We as kids did the flower market with dad every summer and any time we were off school from eight years old until I was twenty one! I don't know how dad adjusted to that schedule his whole life, I never could, because the rest of the week him and mom were cutting flowers from sun up until sundown!

About that time in the seventies and early eighties San Francisco was alive! You had "The Streets of San Francisco" on TV, the big screens were filled with "Dirty Harry" movies, and you had the hippies in the Haight-Ashbury District and the Gay movement was in full swing in the Polk and Castro Districts. Mom and Dad were cranking in the "Green stuff!"

Things drastically changed in the 1990's, by then Reagan created NAFTA which opened the imports from South America which began to flood the flower industry with cheap, beautiful red-stem roses, carnations, gladiolas, and many other flowers and by the mid 1990's all the rose, chrysanthemum, and carnation growers in the Bay Area were out of business. Thanks Ronnie! Mom and Dad's business were mostly flower shippers that shipped our flowers all over the US and NAFTA killed us because the florists now could have flowers directly shipped to them from South America. Thanks Ronnie! In addition the corporate mega supermarkets like K-Mart and Safeway began selling flowers these cheap flowers in the supermarkets and that put out of business most of the little corner flower stalls throughout San Francisco which was the balance of our business. Thanks Ronnie! To make matters worse, the AIDS epidemic hit San Francisco during the late 1980's and most of the 1990's and we lost 75-80 percent of our gay customers., due largely by the delay in Federal funding to find a cure for this epidemic, but instead The Reagan Administration tried to create a quarantine for HIV/AiDS victims, thank God that didn't happen. Thanks Ronnie! Sadly enough I lost my twin brother to this disease in 1997.

During that time with the loss of Larry, and I was in college, Nonno had passed away, Mom and Dad were getting tired of trying to run a twenty one acre farm on their own. It was too much for them. They sold the last flower farm in 1998 and kept the flower stall at the flower market until 2007, when mom fell and broke her hip and dad had to take care of her until her death at 89 in 2014. Dad now lives on the farm here in Sierra Valley and at 92 years old is still farming after all these years!, Outstanding in his field, although now vegetables, not flowers!.

I must say the color of green never crossed my mind in those days because we were a flower farm and blooming ornamental flowers are almost never green, but we did grow some ornamental greens to cut during the off-season. Mostly we had a year round of color on our farm. Spring was full of silver pussy willow, our fields were full of yellow mustard, in-bloom were pink, red and white peach and quince blossoms, cream-colored cherry blossoms, yellow forsythia and lavender/purple lilacs. Then on to summer were fields of coxcomb and celosia with a wide variation of colors, red, yellow, orange, white, and purple along with mixed colors of ornamental sunflowers in colors of yellow, maroon, brown, crimson and Aztec blends, finishing out with ruby globe amaranth and a rainbow of colors in our aster mix. Fall brought on the autumn foliage colors, dad would go out in the forest and cut bows of colored oak , maple and madrone, along with drying a lot of our cockscomb and celosia, selling pumpkins, corn stalks, colored Indian and strawberry corn, and colored gourds.

Winter brought on the collection of all shades of green: pine cones, Christmas trees, wreath bows and winter berries like toyon and mountain ash for Christmas decorations and cutting yellow variegated euonymus, and wild silver pussy willow. Throughout all the seasons the color green was only noticeable around Christmas when the flower market had loads of wreaths, and town was filled with Christmas tree lots.

As for the ornamental greens, when you think of florists and commercial flower growers you think of roses, carnations, chrysanthemums, gladiolas, potted plant growers etc., but there is a specific industry of growers that just grow green foliage plants of all shades of green. The florists use the stems of green foliage shrubs for "filler" in flower arrangements to give some variety and depth to the bouquet or piece. So Dad had small hedges and green plants around the farm and the yard that he would cut and bunch for the flower market, of all shades of green. We grew mock orange, variegated mock orange, pittosporum, boxwood, African boxwood, and euonymus, to name a few. But it's wasn't a big deal in the large picture of the rest of the flowers we grew, it just diversified our crops, and because they were evergreen we could cut off of the shrubs all year long and during times that our other flowers were not in season.

As I think back to Mom and Dad's flower farm, it was quite unique. They made a good living in the heart of Silicon Valley during a time of the largest spread of development and loss of agriculture land in California's history, even after they were taken over twice by eminent domain. What we did in the flower business was special, a lost art. Most growers had hot houses and were growing "typical" flowers roses etc. but the Romano's found a niche of growing what seemed to be normal agricultural fruit trees and unique field crops and turned them into a niche market in the flower industry. Nonno and Dad planted ten acres of a mixture of peach, cherry, and almond trees, not for fruit production but or cut flowers. As a kid I would accompany Nonno, in the orchards and he would graft off the fruiting stems and graft on scions (small growing stems) of double flowering varieties. When these trees were in bloom we had the most impressive orchard in Santa Clara Valley. The famous florist in San Francisco, Podesta & Baldocci would order truckloads of 8-10 foot limbs and decorate Maiden Lane in San Francisco with these tree branches. It was spectacular!

Not only on the farm did we grow unique crops as I mentioned before but we spent a lot of time off the farm cutting wild plants all over California when our farm flowers were out of season. Nonno was the master! Before I was born and Mom and Dad were married, Nonno and Dad would drive the country sides for shrubs and trees in bloom or for their colored foliage value. In the spring they sought out Acacia species for their spectacular yellow foliage, and lilacs, quince and any flowering shrub that would bloom earlier than ours did up in the northern part of the State. Summer time they were too busy on the farm to go out in the country side, but beginning in fall they would hop in the truck and go to the mountains to cut the fall colors of the deciduous trees, then as the holidays came around would cut Christmas trees, and cedar bows for wreath, and pine cones, not loose ones on the ground but attached to the limbs because no one was crazy enough to clime the pine and Redwood trees to do that but Nonno! That was his specialty and trademark at the S.F. Flower Market. Nonno would climb sometimes over 100 feet with a hand saw, pruner and rope and cut the ends of these conifer trees and lower them down to Dad to bundle them and load on the truck. He made good money (the *"green stuff"*) on these for years. After Nonno got old that ended, Dad and I are not fond of heights!

After Christmas and before the blossoms bloomed on the farm Nonno and Dad were off again to the Delta scanning the levies for wild pussy willow, cattails, nutgrass, and wild artichoke (Cardone) flower stalks. They were the ultimate scavengers for anything that was in bloom or different than the norm at the flower market. The florists couldn't wait to see what dad brought to market every week!

That foraging continued well after Nonno died in 1975, and Mom and Dad, kept up the tradition until Dad left the flower market in 2007 I would tell people if you see an old guy and his wife with a small box truck on the side of the road in the middle of nowhere, it was probable Mom and Dad picking some sort of a flower. They could make money on anything even "weeds!"I always said that if the holocaust ever came or Armageddon the only thing left on this planet would be "coyotes, cockroaches, and the Romano's!"

It was quite a contrast when I bought the farm here in Sierra Valley in 1989, something was different here, I was missing all the colors of the flower farm, and now the dominant color was green. My entire vegetables field was missing the colors of the rainbow; that's when I understood that in nature and in general most areas do not have con-centrations of colors like our old flower farms, but instead most vegeta-tion were mostly shades of green, especially here in a harsh climate on my farm thus twenty seven shades of green!

Louis and Rose Romano

Emerald Green

Sierra Valley: My Family Farmstead

"If your knees aren't green by the end of the day you ought to seriously re-examine your life"

Bill Watterson

I chose the color Emerald Green to represent Sierra Valley, My Farmstead. It's the hub of all activity. Emerald green encourages growth and reflection, peace and balance. The color Emerald green suggests the concept of eternity a color that constantly renews itself in nature through generations to come.

Emerald green inspires and creates ideas, creates wellbeing emotionally and spiritually. All farmers are not created equal. Each farm and small farmer has their fingerprint on their piece of land. Agriculture is based on science but farming is the art. The artist is each farmer and their farm is like an artist's canvas, a blank sheet in the beginning and then the farm becomes the art that each farmer creates on his/her land and the end result is them, they become the farm.

Emerald green is the symbol of hope that represents the pioneers and settlers before me (I needed a lot of hope to transform this ranch to a farm). The gemstone Emerald is one of the few stones that symbolically cover a broad range of life's experiences and milestones. It is the stone of prophecy. The color of Emerald green acts as tranquilizer for the troubled mind (that's me! I'll need it to figure this place out!).

In history Emerald green represents a mystery element to it (what was it like when the Jim Beckwourth was exploring Sierra Valley, this unknown region of California) dating back to the belief of the Emerald gemstone and into my generation I want to transform this old "Peter Tumbledown Ranch" (as mom would call this place) into my new farmstead, Sierra Valley Farms.

Sierra Valley: The Jewel of the Sierras as it was first called by the settlers was actually an ancient Lake bed, thousands of years before Jim Beckwourth found his famous Beckwourth Pass. Long before Beckwourth this high alpine valley was inhabited by the Maidu Indians, a peaceful California tribe that spent the harsh winters down around Oroville and the cooler summers in Plumas County to hunt wildlife and fish which was in abundance. The Maidu were the primary Indians in Plumas County until the discovery of the region by the famous fur trapper and trader James P. Beckwourth. Born a slave from an African slave mother and an English father Sir Jennings Beckwith in 1798 in Frederick County Virginia, James Pierson Beckwith, later know as Jim Beckwourth (He decided to change the spelling of his name later in life as it is today the town I live in Beckwourth population 446, elevation 4912 feet) was born.

Jim Beckwourth as a young man left home in 1824 and signed on with General William Ashley for a trapping expedition to the Rocky Mountains. Jim Beckwourth has a flamboyant reputation in history as being quite a "character", he was over six feet tall, a strong man, and liked to wear a lot of "bling" Indian jewelry and gold it was said, he spoke six languages and in 1828 was captured by the Crow Indians and lived with them for many years marrying one of the chief's daughters. He then travelled west trapping in Utah and Wyoming. He was sought after by the early pioneers travelling west to guide their wagon trains because of his knowledge of the mountains and his experiences with dealing with the Indians.

The gold rush attracted Beckwourth to the west and early in 1850 he was prospecting for gold in northern California around Indian Valley (Quincy), Plumas County traveling towards the Pitt River when he saw a pass through the mountains "far away to the southward that seemed to be lower than any other", that pass he named Beckwourth Pass, the gateway to Sierra Valley, which currently is still the lowest pass in the Sierra Nevada Mountain Range (In 1936 Beckwourth Pass was designated as a California Historical monument). In the history journals Beckwourth talked about this beautiful valley he found a few miles to the east, the lowest elevation pass through the rugged Sierra Nevada Mountains, Beckwourth Valley he named it and years later it became Sierra Valley.

This trail to the pass then became the Beckwourth Trail (If only the Donner Party were so lucky five years before, history would be different). The Beckwourth Trail originated in the Truckee Meadows (Sparks, Nevada) and continued over Beckwourth Pass through Sierra Valley, down the Feather River canyon, and ended up in Marysville, California. It's documented that Beckwourth led the first successful intact wagon train into Marysville in 1851. The Beckwourth Trail was used for wagon trains until 1855 when the railroad came into the region, and today the trail is a national landmark.

James P. Beckwourth established a trading post and built a cabin at the northern end of Sierra Valley in Beckwourth. He continued trading and trapping within the West until his death in 1866. He was buried with honors as a celebrated Crow Indian Chief. He was 69 years old. His cabin has been restored and is a historical landmark and has been relocated to a site off of Highway 70 outside of Sierra Valley on the way to Portola, and is open to the public. Beckwourth's findings led to the railroads finding their way to the region in the late 1860-1870's. After the gold rush many settlers remained in the area and because the Sierra Valley was rich in perennial grass rangeland, water, and accessible land that made it attractive to the European immigrants from northern Italy and Switzerland.

The Sierra Valley & Mohawk Railway Company was one of the first companies to come into Sierra Valley with their single narrow gauge rail in 1895. History states that this attracted the larger more sophisticated double rail way lines of Western Pacific Railroad to follow suit in which they installed the Chilcoot Tunnel in 1906 under Beckwourth Pass to get access to Sierra Valley and the Feather River corridor down to Chico, Oroville, and Marysville. With the railroad came the European immigrants. For some reason Sierra Valley attracted those from northern Italy and Switzerland (Swiss-Italian), after visiting our family over there in the Italian Alps I can see why. Farming and ranching practices are pretty much the same because it's cold, at high elevation and it looks the same. Why not just bring your Italian livelihood to America, and they did!

There was a huge influx of Swiss-Italian immigrants coming into the Sierra Valley in the 1870's and 1880's to find work on ranches and develop their own ranches to meet the demands of cream and butter in northern Nevada. . In those early years of Sierra Valley there wasn't any sagebrush as we have today, and the valley floor was mostly pasture of native perennial bunch grasses, buffalo grass, wild clover and wild rye. The early immigrants could see that Sierra Valley had a high potential for raising several types of grain. Specifically winter grain of barley, oats and hard wheat. By 1861 Sierra Valley was shipping tons of hay, barley, oats and wheat to Nevada dairies, to meet the demand for butter in Virginia City and Carson City (*History of Sierra County*: James J. Sinnot). The Cold Brook and Sattley creameries were in full operation by the end of the 1890's. Sierra Valley Creamery in Loyalton, California was the only butter factory in northeastern California.

This article was displayed in the Mountain Messenger local paper in 1870:

SOME ECONOMICS of the VALLEY

Editor Messenger

"...I will in this article give the readers of your paper a few statistics of the Sierra Township.

"There are 22,000 acres enclosed with about 500 miles of fencing.

Nearly 2,500 acres were cultivated in 1870."

RETURNS: From 945 acres of wheat, 13,445 bushels; from 595 acres of oats,
11,785 bushels; From 860 acres of barley, 19,022 bushels and 2400 bushels
Of potatoes.

"We cut last year from 6525 acres, 6,873 tons of hay; 1088 dairy cows
Produced 66,560 pounds of butter and 1,000 pounds of cheese."

"There are in the township 4500 head of cattle, 700 horses and only 12
Mules."

"There are several large bands of sheep grazing here, one of 5,000 head.

"We have about 400 hogs and 2,800 chickens. Average price of chickens
Is $0.50 each. Eggs are $0.28 per dozen."

Butter was the most important dairy product of the Sierra Valley dairies. Milk could not be preserved on a large scale and only a negligible amount of cheese was made, mostly Swiss cheese. Before 1880 the Durham pure-breeds had been the major dairy cow, the principle breeding strain. Only a few herds of pure bred were raised and in most cases Durham bulls were crossed with lower quality stock to produce milking shorthorns. In 1883, the Nevada and Oregon Railroad began carrying Sierra Valley Butter into Reno and three years later, four tons a week were going as far south east to Virginia City.

The Holstein breeding stock was brought into Sierra County 1887 and that became the premier dairy cow of Sierra Valley by 1890. From

1880-1890 is has been documented that Sierra County alone (southern portion of Sierra Valley) had 156 farms ranging from 100-500 acres, with no farms over 1,000 acres. and only twelve contained more than 500 acres. A total of 38,965 acres were being farmed in 1880. Land continued to be purchased under the Desert Culture Act of 1878 and slowly but surely the farms grew in size, and the Swiss-Italian immigrants homesteaded land not already claimed (as my grandfather, Jacamo Folchi did in 1907). As these farms and ranches began to populate Sierra Valley the invention of barbed-wire came about and land owners began to fence off the open range for their livestock in the 1880's.

Irrigation became a growing concern on how to properly manage water for their crops and livestock. In 1881 the Sierra Valley farmers/ranchers began their most impressive experimental effort to find needed water by drilling artesian wells. In 1882 Walter Ede was one of the first to successfully drill an artesian well on the eastern foothills. By 1889 seven hydraulic jetting drills were drilling wells throughout Sierra Valley, and by the 1890's Sierra Valley were peppered with wind-powered pumps (windmills) to bring up the ground water for agriculture.

It is also documented that there were huge grasshopper infestation in the 1880's that decimated grain crops for years in Sierra Valley to the point they contacted Thomas Edison to find an invention to eradicate the pest. This went on for several years and ranchers and dairies were in threat of going out of business by having to burn all their fields. This pest subsided in the late 1880's only to have a plague of rabbits decimate a lot of the grain fields.

As more Swiss-Italian immigrants began to farm and bring livestock into Sierra Valley, this also brought in livestock diseases. In 1888, pink-eye devastated the horse herds killing foals of mares that contracted the disease. That same year a dysentery ailment took its toll of the calf crop and killed a prize Holstein bull in the A.S. Nichol's dairy herd, one of the first Holstein bull brought into Sierra Valley.

During this period between 1880-1890 most of the Sierra Valley

Beef was sold to the miners. The large, English owned, Sierra Buttes, and Plumas-Eureka mines were the heavy buyers, along with supplying the surrounding towns of Downieville, Allegany, Forest City and Sierra City.

Throughout the early 1900's the dairy industry faced lowering prices, heavy competition along with the depression years where the industry could not survive, and by the 1930-1950's there were only a few dairies throughout Sierra Valley. The railroads began to discontinue commodity service lines to the lower big cities of Sacramento, Oakland and San Francisco, which meant the local dairies could no longer get their milk, butter and cheese down to these bigger cities. The Western, Southern and Union Pacific Railroads were all going to interstate freight lines and this became the demise of the dairy industry in Sierra Valley and northern Nevada. Today there are no dairies in Sierra Valley and only a few small "mom and pop" dairies in northern Nevada. The old diary families in Sierra Valley that are still in business and all the other ranchers here are in cow-calf beef and hay operations.

My Family

Family portrait of the Folchi's around 1925

My grandfather, Jacamo Folchi was a Swiss Italian immigrant who migrated to Sierra Valley in 1907. He then wired back to Italy to send a wife, Mary and my family farmstead had begun in Sierra Valley, Plumas County, Beckwourth, California. The Folchi's were "newbies "to Sierra Valley compared to the older families that migrated here in the late 1870's. Between 1910 and 1924 Mary and Jacamo had Dena, the first, and then followed with five boys: Albert, Marion, Raymond, Emilio, and Benny, and the last in 1924 were my mom Rose. By the 1940's Grandpa Folchi had purchased four different ranches adjoining each other encompassing over 3,000 acres. With five boys and two girls, mom being the youngest, they ran a dairy/cattle and hay operation into the late 1970's. Grandpa died young, I never met him, well before I was born, in 1945 on Thanksgiving Day. Dena the oldest girl got married young and moved off the ranch and the boys Albert (Beno), Marion, Raymond, Emilio and Benny, along with mom and Grandma continued the dairy and ranching operations. Grandma died in 1964 when I was only seven, I do remember she made the best berry pies ever, and was very stern, I recall one time my brother Larry was touching something on the stove and she gave his a swift "wack", like batting away a fly, she was a typical Italian grandma, great cook and "as tall as wide!"

The uncles were mountain men, tough to the core and great storytellers. Beno as he was called (Albert) was the oldest, the fabricator, milker, jokester, and the most accident prone...rumor has it he chopped his thumb off cutting wood and the rooster took off with it , then later mowed his toe off on an equipment accident. Beno went into a deep depression after a couple of his brothers died and spent the last 20 years in a convalescent home and died there. You know in those days there were no safety guards on farm equipment and almost every old timer around here is missing some part of their body. The next in line was Marion, he loved to talk, but rumor has it he always tried to get out of haying so one day in his youth he went to jump out of the barn loft and got his foot caught that left him dangling for hours. I guess the brothers just left him there to prove a point! He was in the tank battalion on Monte Cassini in WWII and came home surviving a tank blast, after the war he worked for the Plumas County road department and lived in Beckwourth. Next came my favorite uncle, Raymond, he sported an old leather cowboy hat, thin and always smiling and laughing, he liked to bake and tend to the animals, the gardener. He was the butcher and sent us wonderful Italian-Swiss sausage links during the holidays. There was always a crowd around Raymond because he was the best storyteller of the bunch. Never married and died young of a heart attack. Next in line was Emilio, who I bought the ranch from, he and I are a lot alike, and would get together frequently to go hunting and fishing. He was very educated, self-taught, the "brains" of the Folchi ranch, high strung, opinionated but hilarious! Another great story teller that survived WWII, a hunter, could build anything and a thinker. He lived with his wife Betty, and after I bought the ranch they moved to Portola. Emilio passed away at 93 in 2014 a few months before mom. The youngest brother was Benny he was short and stocky, the horseman, and "bull" of the brothers always had a chuckle, and a logger. I remember he would leave at 5am and come home from logging at 6pm in his gray-striped logger shirt, silver hard hat with these "car hart-like" faded black pants, with steel-toed boots all covered in soot and forest dust, just like a coal miner with just the whites of his eye like high beams looking at you, and a big smile with his teeth covered in pine dust. He was tough with hands like leather and a strong grip. Once he cleaned up he was a horseman in an ironed shirt, Stetson cowboy hat, silver-rodeo belt buckle in wrangler jeans with fancy cowboy boots and ready for the town! Sadly, Benny died young of a logging accident in 1970. Last was mom and she stayed on the ranch with grandma until she married dad in 1956. After Uncle Benny and Raymond died in the early seventies three of the four ranches were sold and just 65 acres of the Dekker Ranch that Uncle Emilio and Aunt

Betty lived on was left.

Like most other small farms that have been around for generations, these stories and recollections keep the spirit of farming alive not only amongst the farming families but hopefully inspire young people and those who are tired of their dead end jobs to look at a new way of life from the urban and suburban doldrums, if nothing else to start attending farmers markets and building relationships with local small farmers and supporting the local food movement.

It was Labor Day weekend around 1969 and we came to the farm as we did every Labor Day for a long weekend. All the cousins came to the ranch (David, Jack, Kathy, Virginia, Marie, Delisa, and Jana) and the Uncles would BBQ a lamb up at the old Vesti Nelson Ranch (one of the other ranches they owned) about a mile away. This ranch was my favorite. It had a beautiful canyon between these two incredible rock uplifts that jetted out of the ground soaring up over 500 feet. There were springs and a great view of Sierra Valley below, on this particular weekend we brought up our mini-bike to cruise the ranches. Everyone seemed to be in a big "party mode"…we spent the day up on the mountain with my cousins eating, drinking, playing and riding the mini-bikes. At the end of the day we all came back to the farm except Dad, Uncle Beno, and my cousin Jim Avila about two hours later Mr. Erwin (who lived on the farm in a huge trailer) came speeding down the driveway, dust a flyin' and came to a screeching halt, the doors flew open broadcasting bellows of laughs as Dad, Uncle Beno and Jim Avila stumble out of the four-door Ford truck "drunk-as-a-skunk", Dad never drank much and Larry and I had never seen him drunk before, and boy did they "get an ear full" from their wives!! It was always fun times at the ranch.

Every time we came up to visit on Labor Day weekend the uncles would take us fishing, either down in the meadow to catch bullhead catfish, or trout fishing at a neighboring mountain lake. I loved to go fishing and hunting with my uncles, and cousins David and Virginia.

They were our age, and my twin brother Larry was not too fond of hunting and fishing, but would rather rummage through the ranches looking for old relics. He was an "old-soul" and loved antiques, of all kinds, especially old people. He could sit and talk to the elderly for hours mesmerized by their stories of the past. On this day in 1970, they had just opened Lake Davis about 10 miles from the ranch here where I live, so my uncle Marion agreed to take Larry and me, David and Virginia fishing at the new lake. Upon arrival, Lake Davis was packed with fisherman, shoulder-to-shoulder. We found a clear spot along the shore and began "rigging up" our spinning reels with a rapala (fake minnow) lure. David, Virginia and I began catching some nice 20 inch rainbow trout right away. Larry was having trouble getting his "rigging" set-up, so Uncle Marion helped him get going. Larry had an accident when he was about 10 years old on an old playground slide that tore his tendons in his throwing arm (right), so his throwing motion had been hampered. On top of that Larry was never the athletic type and hated all sports, which didn't help matters any. On his first cast, as he swung his fishing rod to cast the lure out to the Lake, he released the bail (mechanism that releases the fishing line) too early, and the lure rigging hit a jeep behind him, thus breaking the trajectory, and as he casted forward, the lure flew forward and ended up protruding into the back of his head. A fishing lure has two huge treble hooks that are gnarly enough to take out of a fish's mouth let alone trying to get one out that's embedded in your skull. The fun was just beginning. Luckily it was the back of his head and not in eye or face area, but we couldn't get it out, so we clipped off the lure and off to the Plumas County hospital we went. Well of course it was a Sunday, and they only had one old nurse on duty that was half blind, so to make a long story short... she shaved the wrong part of his head first, and gave him too much local anesthesia that numbed his whole face that he could hardly talk. In the end she finally got the lure out but Larry had a scar there for years. That was the last day Larry ever went fishing!

My Farmstead: Sierra Valley Farms

It was 1989 when I got the call at my Parks & Recreation office at Lake Tahoe from my aunt Betty and uncle Emilio that they couldn't keep up with the ranch anymore because it was too much work for the two of them and if I wanted to buy it. They sold all the cattle, and auctioned off the equipment and offered the ranch to me. It was an empty shell, "a ranch without a shovel", and "yes" I said in a moment of sudden impulse... I was happy to purchase it for $175,000.

So what did I just do? Have I lost my mind? I just gave up an eighteen year career in Parks & Recreation at Lake Tahoe, which I spent eight years in college and received a master's degree, and now I've bought my uncle's dilapidated old dairy farm. Are you sure you want to do that? After all that hard work as a kid on the flower farm I swore I'd never farm again...well I guess the fruit doesn't fall from the tree afterwards. Yep in 1989 I took the plunge back into farming but this time it was for native plants and vegetables, not flowers. At least I hope.

On my first day of owning the new farm in July of 1989, my Farmstead (Sierra Valley Farms), and I traveled to the farm to reflect on the fun times on this ranch. I started walking around looking at all the outbuildings that I remembered as a child. They were all here, half falling down, with old, rusted tin steep-pitched roofs, and hand-split wooden siding, just as I remembered them. *The ranch house*, a small two bedroom farm house that Grandma, Uncle Raymond, Beno, and Benny lived in(these uncles were bachelors)that grandma cooked so many wonderful meals; *the granary*, which was out by the road that housed thrashings of wheat, barley, and oats; *the dairy*, a small wooden shack that the walls were starting to separate, had a crude concrete floor with a small raised concrete pad that the milk separator sat on when the uncles would separate the milk and the cream; *the pig shed*, across from the hay barn and still had two feet of manure compacted to the ground with three different compartments that pigs used to get out of the weather. I remember when I was only about ten Larry and I would help Uncle Beno feed the pigs. We would get a bucket of "slop" (bucket of grain from the granary and a bucket of sour milk) and pour them into these home-made troughs (small boiler tanks cut in half about six feet long and six inches deep) and all the pigs would come running snorting and jumping in feet first "slopping it down"; *the hay barn*, the one big one next to the pig shed blew down in a strong winter wind storm about five years before I bought the ranch, but the smaller one is still in good shape, it was the feeding barn in the winter and for hay storage; the *chicken house*, along the drive as you entered, loved this one, built like a fort to keep the weasels and varmints out… "you know everything likes chicken", and had side doors to the hens nests so you could open them and get the eggs without going into the chicken house; *the nursery*, was attached to the car garage that my Emilio made for Aunt Betty when she opened a small plant nursery selling annual bedding plants to the locals; *the wood shed*, was a "lean-to" building with an open front next to *the well house*; two well houses actually, one housed the house well, and one was a hand-dug well for the animal troughs; *the bunkhouse*, the bunkhouse a small one-room shack with a wood stove that was used by the Uncles to make cheese, cut up meat, make sausage and bottle milk; *the garage*; *the shop*; and who could forget *the outhouse*, a two-seater pit toilet next to the tool shed. Not sure what the logic was, if any, but I guess if you gotta-go, but your tool in the shed and do your business! I call it the first unisex bathroom in Plumas County because if you're in there and the next person needs to go there was another seat right next to you, it didn't matter what gender you were in those days. I bet there was some good conversation over the years, if only the walls could talk. But in reality if you had to go in January when it was ten below zero I don't think you stayed in there very long and you didn't care who was next to you!

All the buildings had been painted red (except the house) years before when a transient salesman came through and gave the uncles "Have I got a deal for you…a deal you can't refuse" that he would paint every building for one low price and they fell for it. That fall when the rains came the paint was a red "white -wash" that dissolved in water and it's said that when the sheep ran under the eaves to get out of the rain they rubbed the red white-wash all over them turning the herd pink! Today only the faded red paint remains on the barn and few outbuildings.

What I love about Sierra Valley and this farm is that there is so much history about this valley, the pioneers, the Swiss Italian immigrant settlers and my family creating this farmstead. Now I can call this ranch my own and someday pass on my legacy to my future generations, or at least offer it to them. This is my new home and I am going to continue on as a third generation Romano farmer, at least I hope! As I finished my self-guided tour of my new farm I realized that I was really "green." I haven't farmed in over 20 years since I left the flower farm and that was under Dad's direction. I had never farmed before by myself and on top of that I had no idea how to farm in the mountains or even what would grow here. A total "green horn!"

As a boy, I remember, Uncle Beno getting up at 4am on a Christmas weekend to go out in below zero weather to milk five cows, break ice (in the water troughs), then feed the chickens, goats, hogs, lambs, horses and cows, come in for a late breakfast around 10am, then go onto "ranch activities", come in for grandma's late lunch…take a break in early afternoon…then go back out in the evening and do it all over again, plus putting the chickens in for the night.

So do I want to deal with livestock every day for the rest of my life, or do I want to work as hard every day as Mom and Dad did in the flower business dealing with crops? First of all I've never been fond of big animals like horses, ponies, donkeys, cows, pigs, sheep or goats, but we had chickens, dogs and cats and I can deal with those on the farm. So I guess my decision was easy, "hey, with plants they don't have attitudes and quarks like animals and in the fall you just disk and plow them under and be done with them till spring", so easy decision...crops, "I just gotta figure out what grew here! "In past history the early settlers did grow potatoes and beets and Uncle Raymond had a great garden behind the bunkhouse that I would help him pick Swiss chard, carrots, lettuces, radishes for our dinners. There was also a big rhubarb plant by the bunkhouse and he would pick the stalks to bake rhubarb pie for Thanksgiving. So I know I can start with those cool season crops.

So it became, Sierra Valley Farms, Occupation: Farmer. Every farmer goes through the jubilation in the beginning of how they would like to set up their farm, and I was no different. It was just I was trying to develop a vegetable farm in one of the harshest places in the West and it wasn't going to be easy.

I went through growing pains in the 1990's looking for an identity, and trying to financially sustain the farm. We were "robbing Peter-to-pay-Paul" well into 2005, my wife at the time, Kim and I birthed a new son Joey in summer of 1998 and my previous steady paycheck from Truckee Parks & Recreation was long gone and my side business of native plants and erosion control work had exhausted all the local jobs, so I had to find a steady stream of income or we would lose the farm. Tensions were high in the family unit and it seemed like every winter I was trying to come up with "another get-rich-quick scheme", and Kim was tired of hearing it. She'd say "you're in denial...all the projects and extra income schemes just cost us more money, and you have to go to your dad and have him bail us out." She was right, I was. I was running out of options. Sometimes having "no money" is good because we were broke and we didn't have money to improve the buildings that were here on the farm. The Farmstead was just as "broken-down", if not more with another fifteen years of age, than when I bought it. So my solution to financial sustainability was right in front of my eyes, here on the farm, and I didn't even see it.

About 2007, the organic movement in northern California was, I believe, at its most contagious and popular stage for chefs, restaurants, farmers markets and CSA's as ever. I was working with a wonderful, "trend-setting" young chef named Mark Estee and we had established a restaurant CSA with his restaurant Moody's Bistro & Lounge in Truckee, and at that time we started a farm stand with our fresh organic produce and from other farms, by remodeling the old granary to a farm stand in 2005. Estee called me one day and said

"Hey Gar... (In his Boston accent) I got this gig to put on a benefit dinner to raise money for Project Mana (food bank in Truckee)...I need a place to have it. Do you have any place on the farm?" I said

"You know I have this old barn that I never use in the summer, it just sits here and then I pack it full of equipment in the winter to get them out of the snow...let's do in there!"

We did and it was a huge success and everybody loved it! Mark and I then started a summer series "Dinner in the Barn", once a month for three months during the summer which continues today, and has made the "Top 10 Things to do in Lake Tahoe", according to the locals.

That opened my eyes to every building on the farm...thus came agritourism to save the day! Well it didn't save the day, but it was a focus in the right direction to help save the farm. We continued to struggle, limping along, leaking oil, on four bald tires, and a slipping clutch...Kim finally got tired of dealing with the farm and moved on... and I'm still looking for that "golden wand" to bring the farm past the finish line.

The farm is ever evolving; nothing is status quo on a farm. It's alive and changing constantly. No matter how good your business plan is there will always be a need to expand the farm with another crop-another source of income because there are always unexpected cost and you must have a contingency plan, plan A,B, C.... Throughout my years of farming, on the flower farm and here on my farm I've learned that, "shit happens", most of the time by mistake or it's been staring you in the face for years and all of a sudden the light goes on..."shit, why didn't I think of that before!" That's what happens here on the farm all the time! Every farm and farmer goes through it and those who can't adapt and mitigate problems will fall by the wayside.

It's funny how things work, I don't think anyone realizes how tough the learning curve is as a farmer, it takes time and every day you learn something new, you have these grandiose ideas of what you're going to do on your farm and it's going to be this great success story, but you're dealing with mother nature and you can lose, lose and lose, time after time, because it's not what you think it ought to be, but nature dictate how it will be, and the trick is to learn how it will be.

It's funny to me, despite our struggles, we've come a long way here on the farm since that first day, and somehow I'm still farming after all these years. Being a third-generation farmer and barely surviving the first fifteen years here I've realize that most of my customers have no clue how difficult it is to make a living farming. People are clueless about what farmers do, and in general, have no clue where their food comes from, especially how hard it is to make a living at farming. They take it for granted that the food just shows up at the Supermarket! I work 16 hours a day, every day is a Monday, there are no perks, and you're on call 24 hours. This farm becomes me, I become the farm, it's part of you because you are the artist that painted this Muriel and if the farm fails, I've failed. I care more about the farm than me.

So after the Project Mana dinner, I looked at the farm differently, not only at the crops that I'd been focusing on since that day in 1989 when I bought the ranch, but at the Farmstead itself. The Farmstead includes everything on the farm, buildings, crops, equipment, and other features to include: the incredible 360 degree panoramic view, the old abandoned highway (my current driveway) that Chloe and I take our morning walk, and the occupation of being a farmer. I realized farmers have become a mystic ...few and far between. I needed to attract people to the farm because of the whole picture, and charge them for it!

Again only one percent of all American occupations according to the U.S. Census Bureau are full-time farmers. We're the Farmasaur! Well shit....let's make this place "Jurassic Farm!!" So let's do it! After that benefit dinner here on the farm, the common denominator is that most people have "green with envy" over farmers. It's pretty cool to be a farmer these days especially an organic one. People want to come and visit the farm and see what a farmer does, because it sounds glamorous, and few people today have access to a farm. Most people are two to three generation removed from a family member that was a farmer let alone one that actually had a garden.

Since that light has gone on in 2007, we have opened the farm to agritourism events to help diversify our farm. As of 2018 we have expanded our farm stand to a full blown certified Farmers market which has over 20 vendors "a one-stop shop" for locals and a "destination" market for tourists from the Reno/Tahoe area for 16 weeks during the summer that attracts over 500 people to our farm every Friday. It's is the only on-farm certified Farmers market in California. We have expanded our "Dinner in the Barn Series" to include an Executive chef featuring a different guest chef every month, and a featured winery, for an all-inclusive price that includes a four-course family-style dinner and farm tour. Utilizing our empty pastures for parking and easy access to our Farmers market area, taking advantage of our panoramic views and spectacular Sierra sunsets we created the "Food, Blues & Views", Summer Blues, Concert Series featuring iconic and local blues artists from around the country, with a gourmet food truck, once a month, three in all during the summer evenings. Last we have created a hop garden in our old native plant shade structure, and have been growing hops for a local brewery, who have named the local IPA brew after Dad, calling it a "Louie" for October Fest. We have over 30 volunteers that help pick hops around Labor Day and we provide a keg of beer from the brewery, and pizza's in return for brewery giving us kegs of beer for our events. In all we now attract over 6000 people to our farm over the summer months.

The farmstead has become the main attraction that is now supplemented by my twenty-seven shades of green. It's my Emerald green gemstone. In addition my organic farmstead has "gone green." We are 90% sustainable on solar energy and use the earth' temperature (Geoexchange) to heat our greenhouse, along with four passive solar hoop houses that allow us to grow year round, and being organic we only cover-crop (composting in place) and rotate our fields to maintain our fertility and organic matter, not applying any inputs in over 20 years.

Grandpa Jacamo Folchi you would be proud that an agricultural conservation easement on the farmstead has now been purchased by the Feather River Land Trust, keeping it an organic farm for perpetuity.

Sierra Valley Farms

Twenty-Seven
Shades of Green

Green Acres

"Life expectancy would grow by leaps and bounds if green vegetables smelled as good as bacon."

Doug Larson

The evening of June 12, 2004 a Saturday was gorgeous, I walked out at sunset to view my "green acres" as I do most evenings with cocktail to see what I need to pick for the upcoming week and for some reason the sunlight was just right and I noticed all these shades of green in my vegetable fields which I never really paid attention to before, there was about an acre so far "Yea…that's my niche growing cool season green crops during the summer months when everyone else at the farmers markets are from the hot foothills and Sacramento Valley with tomatoes, squash, beans, corn etc. with warm season crops that I can't grow, but I can grow the cool season crops.

After that day and throughout the season of 2004 everything I looked at was green, green, green, and greener. Not only the crops I planted were green, but all the weeds were green: mallow, pigweed, amaranth, chickweed, dandelion, filaree and nightshade. Everything was GREEN, except my yellow sunflowers. I love my shades of green so much that at the farmers markets the call me "the lettuce guy", the green grocer, or the "the greens guy." Yes my booth has many shades of green, speckled in with colorful radishes, and rainbow carrots.

On one of my last mornings of the season in 2004 in mid-October, I laughed and said to myself "I wonder how many shades of green are out here?" Ten, twenty…and I was curious because each crop variety had a little different shade that made the field look amazing, like "green fields forever" against the perennial pasture as far as the eye could see, so how many different shades of green were there?. They were so prevalent in my "five acres of green". I proceeded to count all the varieties that I had planted that year, that I still do today, and sometimes few more or a few less, but the total was 27 different shades of green. The shades of all my vegetables (as close as I can come to identifying my colors of green) are:

Toscano kale-*Jade green*; red Russian kale-*teal green*; curly kale-*Kelley green*; carrot tops-*jungle green*; beet tops-*myrtle green*; arugula-*moss green*; romaine-*sea green*; spinach-*hunter green*; leaf lettuces-*spring green*; mustard green-*bright green*; radish tops- *dull green*; Swiss chard- *emerald green*; broccoli- *forest green*; asparagus-*olive green*; mint- *mint green*; green cabbage- *sage green*; collard greens-*light green*; Napa cabbage-*lime green*; broccoli raab- *shamrock green*; celery-*celery green*; Italian parsley-*army green*; chicory-*clover green*; plantain-*pea green*; sorrel-*pear green*; cilantro-*olive green*; watercress-*military green*; and green onion-*tule green*, all green, green, green of all shades.

It's the amazing ability of green plants to convert light energy, water, carbon dioxide, and minerals into oxygen (photosynthesis), thus the green pigment in all green plants (chlorophyll) is responsible for the absorption of this light energy for photosynthesis to occur and create plant life. So what makes all these shades of Green? In the color spectrum, if you mix blue and yellow you get green, and if you mix light, medium and dark colors of blue and yellow you get different shades of green, way more than twenty seven. In nature most of the colors are blues (water and the sky) and, yellow-to-orange (sun) which gives us the greens and browns in the world around us today. It is very evident in the Sierra Nevada Mountain Range, the more water, sun, and blue sky the lusher the greens and browns of the meadows and the trees, while if you take away the water you lose the lush vegetation and things turn to gray, very similar to what we see as we go east towards the arid desert. You lose the water and you basically lose the green.

Going into the planting season is my favorite time of year here. Finally getting out of the hard winter "dull-drums", of the frozen tundra from December through February where you spend your days shoveling and plowing snow, chipping ice at all the doors to make sure they don't freeze shut overnight, and insulate water pipes in the well houses and greenhouse and add heat tape and incandescent light bulbs to keep them just above freezing. March and April kind of sucks because winter is never officially over, you'll get nice days, then twelve to fourteen inches of snow then three to five days of rain, then a week of dry, cold, super windy weather, that looks good from the kitchen window, but you freeze your ass off in a half hour trying to work in it. Then comes May, "the teaser"...Ah, summer if finally on it way...NOT!" You'll get three weeks of fabulous weather, no frost in the morning and 75-80 degree days, so that's when "you go for it", and I plant my greens , then around Memorial Day "ZAP...a 26 degree morning, without warning", and you hope for the best on your little seedlings. Like many years here in Sierra Valley we may only have July and winter, and sometimes we get frost every month of the year.

Usually sometime in mid-April I get out in the fields and check the moisture in the soil, driving a shovel in the field and bringing up a clump to see if it sticks to the shovel or not (very high-tek!). If it does it's too wet, if it crumbles off the shovel it's time to "open up" the soil with the disk (which is an implement that has a series of cupped-disks that as you pull it cuts down in the soil and turns over the soil about 10 inches deep), and then get ready to plant. This day it was ready! I went an attached the disk to the tractor and made one-pass with the disk, thus opening up the soil then allows the winds of April to dry out the soil enough that I can plant in about three days if the weather is right. It was, so I prepped the soil for seeding and seeded about a quarter of an acre of a lot of cool season crops, much more than ever before.

My program is to seed a quarter of an acre of the same cool season crops in succession every fifteen days, with the last seeding in late August, which gives me about five acres of vegetables to harvest between June and October for my markets. So for April-August I seeded a lot crops together every two weeks, Three kinds of kale (curly, toscano, red Russian); radishes; carrots; beets; leaf lettuces (spring mix, romaine); arugula; spinach; mustard greens; Swiss chard; broccoli; green cabbage; Napa cabbage; collard greens; broccoli raab; plantain, and green onions. Along the perimeter I line these fields with asparagus; mint; celery; Italian parsley; sorrel; chicory; cilantro and experimented with watercress in a wet drainage ditch.

Usually the first harvest is of greens and radishes that begin around the first week in June and then the rest of the crops follow. Between May and June we do a big assault on the weeds to get them under control before they get out of control, and we were on it that year! It's "asses and elbows", that's all you see for hours on end, until the weeds are gone. Well they're never really gone, just managed.

Since 2004 I have continued to grow my 27 shades of green on my five acres here on the farm expanding to year round, with four hoop houses so that I can continue to grow greens indoors from October through March to supplement my outdoor "greens." Other green favorites that I've added to my crops include: microgreens, wasabi, horseradish, hops, potatoes, sweet green peppers, cucumbers, and salad tomatoes. To this day Sierra Valley Farms greens are cherished by chefs and featured throughout the restaurants and natural food stores in the Reno/Tahoe and Truckee area. In Sierra Valley we are blessed with alluvial soils (because it was an ancient lake bed), and fertility and organic matter from the old corrals of the dairy ranch that left over 50 years of animals (manures) on this ground. Our native soils and wells are high in minerals and in our northern area of Beckwourth we have high amounts of boron, which benefit annuals like vegetables that thrive for that mineral. The mineral boron when taken up by leafy greens and root crops, (beets, radishes, turnips, carrots, potatoes, onions etc.) increases the flavor, longevity and color of the vegetable, which might explain why the vivid shades of green are so distinct and vibrant here on the farm. If you really want to learn about the climate of the Sierra Nevada Mountain Range get a copy of my last *book July and Winter: Growing Food in the Sierra* it has all the details about successfully growing food in the Sierra!

These green acres of all shades of green brighten up this mountain farm and its produce brings joy and nourishment to the surrounding communities of the high Sierra. Not only has it brought a joy and income to sustain this farmer but the different shades of green help keep this farmer in a great mood by appreciating what nature has to offer in this inclement climate.

Olive Green

Farming in Chaos

"An optimist is a person who sees green light everywhere; while a pessimist sees only the red stoplight... the truly wise person is colorblind."

Albert Schweitzer

The color olive is a symbol of peace. Olive is a symbol of strength and of character, with it that can overcome adversity to develop an understanding and caring of the feelings of others, to overcome feelings of deceit and treachery, not blaming others for its problems. That is why I selected the color olive to represent the wide variety of chaotic situations that occur on a daily basis in farming and how we overcome the adversity.

The word Chaos in the Webster Dictionary derives from a Greek word "chasm" or "void" refers to a formless state of matter before the cosmos were created. Chaos is defined as something in complete disorder and confusion; in disarray; total mayhem; complete pandemonium; creating havoc; in turmoil; or in an uproar. It's' behavior is so unpredictable as to appear random, lack of organization and in utter chaos—Farming.

In farming, us small farmers face a number of challenges and chaos can rear its ugly head like the "Green-eyed Monster" anywhere and at any time, and create havoc in the family; on financial matters; dealing with weather conditions (Mother Nature); work crews; crops; and in many other forms. Like the old saying "If anything can go wrong, it usually will go wrong." Like most farmers our farm growing up was no different. Not to mention the out-of-our-control constraints we face like no loans being available, a divisive Schedule Form "F" that is exactly what it stands for (Fuck the Farmer), and numerous useless regulations and obstacles that are intended to make small farmers fail.

Working with Mom and Dad on the flower farm seemed to go so smooth. There were a few 'bumps in the road" that I can remember like the truck broke down or the tractor wouldn't start, but I never remember missing a 2:00 am market in San Francisco (shit... I could have used a few sleep ins!). Things just seem to purr along but I'm sure there were tough times it's just that I was young and didn't see it. It was a different era then, things and times were different in the 1960's -1970. Everyone at the flower market was full-time flower growers, of all ethnics, that were their livelihood. They didn't have jobs off the farm like today to make ends meet or support the farm. They all looked the same and talked the same "flower language", and had the family with them, Mom, Dad, kids, grandpa or grandma or both and any relative that could help. They all had the family unit. Our situation was no different, grandpa lived next store, helping at the farm along with Mom, Dad, Larry and me. It was like spokes in a wheel. Mom didn't drive and she went everywhere with Dad, carrying every bunch of flowers that he ever cut. The only time she wasn't with him was at 2 am at the flower market, because she stayed home to take care of us kids and get us off to school, otherwise she was at Dads side. It's amazing to me how much work we got done as a family of four (five sometimes when Nonno was younger). I think most farmers then worked in a "organized chaos" environment where shifting priorities, putting out spot-fires, and having loss of crops and disengaged employees or family members was normal, they actually didn't even recognize it was chaos—It was farming as usual! In years past most farmers had the family unit. Something myself and most modern day farmers don't have today, and most obvious between my organic vegetable farm versus Dads flower farm. Growing up we had the family unit working together and it helped to minimize chaos because we all were on the same page, like a fine tuned machine, (even though I know a lot of families don't and even create more chaos).

In today's generation it's different, everyone kind of goes their own way, with the influence of social media, reality TV and the technical advancement of our electronics i.e. cell phones, iPod, and iPad families are more independent than ever. Even though we live in a rural Plumas County in Beckwourth with only 400 people, (Joeys, Portola High School graduation class of 45 students), my son Joey still had the influences of the large suburban city millennials. Joey wears the same styles, talks the same lingo, listens to the same music, and follows the social media. That makes it hard to get him involved in a farming situation that none of his friends are exposed to, or most likely ever will be exposed to. Over the years, I've become a one-man-army or more like a three - ring circus; me, myself, and I, and I don't have the working family unit that Mom and Dad had with the luxury of all of us working on the farm. Labor is what kills a small farm, so without a family unit, you have to be creative on how you bring in your labor force, most times its utter chaos trying to get production out of unskilled labor. You better have high dollar crops to pay skilled hired help if you're going to go that route. That model is not sustainable for small farms in today's world. To succeed today you still have to do it the old-fashion way of doing most of it by you, and with family and friends and most times that's not possible. I've come to the conclusion that being a single farmer, not farming within a family unit, I'm unlike my parents and farmers of their generation operating their farms in "organized chaos", I operate my farm in a "controlled-chaos" environment. Whereby my farm operation looks out of control (visually and on paper) but which actually functions according to unseen rules of organization. Yea…

that's exactly Sierra Valley Farms!

For example: It had stormed all Friday night, I could hear wind howling, so I got up about 6 am to make some coffee and plan my long day that I knew was ahead of me of clearing snow. Earlier that week we had a break in the weather and had four feet of snow on the ground, at least no snow was predicted for the rest of the week, but bitter cold, so Kim (my wife at the time) with my son Joey drove down to her folks in Auburn, California for the holidays to get out of the cold, snowy weather. It was December of 2009, and was the coldest I had experienced in the ten years that I'd been on the farm. Prior to them leaving we began to drop down to zero, and with the "window of opportunity" I said,

"You and Joey better get over the summit before it snows again, because we're supposed to get another three feet at the end of the week...I'll try to meet you down there when the weather breaks for Christmas."

After they left on that Monday, each day got progressively colder, Tuesday was minus five; Wednesday was minus twelve; Thursday was minus eighteen; and Friday was minus twenty one. As I went to make the coffee, I turned on the water faucet in the kitchen and there was no water, cold or hot, over the course of the week's minus temperatures the permafrost had frozen the house up.

No toilet, no shower, no water. "Ah shit... (I notice I say that a lot in farming)!"

So I thought what else froze?

What about my well house... Greenhouse?

I'd better go check. I looked at the thermometer and it was minus 23, (still the coldest day on record here at the farm), so I bundled up! Put on my thermal underwear, sweats, insulated coveralls, scarf, full hood-wool cap, and my heavy down coat, with two layers of wool socks and my insulated snow boots and gloves. About this time the sun was coming up (which is always the coldest time of the morning) and as I opened the back door of the mud room I noticed that we got about three feet of snow that night and it was pushed against the storm door. I grabbed the snow shovel and I was able to push the door enough to squeeze my way into the "heavy, wet snow." I had to get to the shop and get the bobcat skid loader out to start plowing snow, so that I could get to the well house and green house to see if they were frozen too. It was really cold, and shoveling as fast as I can, it was a lot of work to move that heavy snow. I had to be careful not to sweat too much because my nostrils and forehead were freezing up. It was so cold, my breath was steaming so much that I could hardly see and the cold air was freezing my lungs. I could feel my skin under my wool hood starting to tighten up and my eyelids felt like they were stationary. I made it to the shop and the rolling door was frozen, with the ice pick next to the door (which I leave it there for that reason), I used it to pound on the door to break the ice, chipped away at the base, and was able to get the door open. My shop is the original shop my uncle Emilio built in the 1950's, all green metal sheeting and no insulation. I swear it was colder in there than outside. My Bobcat was an older model from 1979, and in those years there wasn't a block heater that came with tractors that would pre-heat the engine to make it easier to start on cold mornings. Boy did I learn the hard way! Of course with those temperatures the Bobcat would hardly turn over, the battery was new but I could tell that the cold had solidified the oil restricting the engine to turn over. I remember the uncles telling me about these cold times, when they're old tractors wouldn't start they would light a small fire under the oil pan to heat them up from underneath then they would start. Well I may be Italian, but I wasn't gonna try that trick and start the bobcat on fire...all I could visualize was me burning down the shop and all that goes with it! That would be total mayhem! I did have a small propane torch and thought I'd give that a try with a small flame and carefully! After about twenty minutes of lying on that frozen tundra gravel floor, my fingers were numb, and I was *"green around the gills"* feeling the chill, that was enough for me, so I shut off the torch and left the hot oil pan sit for a few minutes while I went back out to clear the snow off the truck and see if it would start, so I could climb inside and warm me up. Of course the truck wouldn't start, none of my vehicles started that day. To shorten a long story, the well house and green house were frozen and the micro greens that I had growing in the green house all froze even with heaters. The Bobcat did start and I was able to plow the snow and get the roadway open, but the house stayed frozen for eleven days in which the power went out for four of those days and without a generator I lit candles, buried all the meat from the freezer deep in the deep snow until the power came on, and kept the wood stove going to heat the house, cook my food and even melted snow in a pot on the stove to pour water in the toilet so it could be used. Luckily I had a lot of booze and canned food. It was the craziest two weeks of utter chaos I had ever spent on the farm. That's the farm life in the mountains. The days did warm up and all the pipes broke in the well house and the green house that I had to repair, but luckily the house thawed out ok. I never did make it down for Christmas or New Years that year. I was just happy to see 2010! Just another chaotic day in winter!

As if farming in the High Sierra isn't challenging in enough you have to contend with the "Queen of Chaos" Mother Nature! She is here on the farm every day to throw a wrench in your works, and can turn the farm into complete pandemonium, whether you like it or not. Testing my wit and patience, and challenging me to a duel on every-thing I do. Despite her efforts to thwart my progress here on the farm, I'm still farming after all these years!

Sierra Valley is the highest alpine valley above 5000 feet elevation in the western Hemisphere, a little larger than Lake Tahoe and about an hour from it. Because of these large land expansions, surrounded by mountains, Sierra Valley can create its own weather with tons of little micro climates with in the valley. So I deal with all of "her" insecurities and "mood swings" on a daily basis. I've had wind storms that have torn off tins off of my roof tops, sucked up umbrellas from my farmers market fifty feet in the air and left them in trees or spit them out, harpooning them through my hoop houses. She has taken the end of my T-Tape (drip tubing) and unraveled almost the whole roll across the valley floor, and rattled this old ranch house like it was going to spin away like the Wizard of Oz. I've had lightning storms that hit the house and blew the old wall phone across the room and fried all my appliances twice since I've been here. She has a wide variety of mood swings, creating total turmoil on farming operations, especially in spring and summer; she can be cold as ice in the morning at twenty six degrees and by mid-afternoon she can get hot at a boiling 100 plus degrees. It's nothing to see a sixty degree mood swing in one day. She likes to tease me though, in May she'll be sweet for about three weeks all "comfy" giving me mild mornings and beautiful eighty degree days so I can get excited about summer coming and plant my first few crops of greens, then about memorial day she starts getting "crotchety", and mad at me for some reason and when I'm ready to pick my first greens she'll say "well take this...you SOB! ZAP comes a twenty seven degree morning to try and kill my new little seedling, but I've out fooled her this time because my twenty seven shades of greens can handle her little antics!

Mother Nature in the Sierra is very neurotic, a "space cadet", the Queen of Chaos can never make up her mind, she wants to be cold in the summer, and I tell her "no you're supposed to be hot"; then she wants warm and dry in the winter, and I say "No...you're supposed to be cold and snowy"...then she cries (rain), and cries, and cries in the spring. She cried so much last winter and spring that she had almost flooded me out! We were like a lake front; the river came up over eight feet! I had a foot of water in the barn and three feet of water in my lower hoop house. Why she even flooded out the muskrats from the river and they burrowed into my flooded hoop house and ate all my radishes under water. She got scolded for that big time!!

Mother Nature does dictate my daily activities wreaking havoc on the farm because as the saying goes "if you don't like the weather in the Sierra, just wait five minutes and it'll change", and people say that for a reason it does change. I've had southwest wind in the morning and north wind in the afternoon on the same day, during the winter the westerly's begin in the morning and then the bitter cold east wind blows in the afternoon. For the first twenty five years that I lived here on the farm I considered our climate to be about like Tahoe/Truckee. Our winters were as cold, but with not as much snow, and the summers like Tahoe temperatures. Over the last five years the weather is changing, especially during the summer months. We used to be in the mid-to-high eighties most of the summer with a few days in the nineties and once in a great moon we would reach 100. I keep extensive weather logs, it's kind of fun because the weather changes so much, and we're on a new heat-wave pattern. We have progressively been getting hotter during the summer, this farm is being affected by climate change!.

We've gone from six days (which was the average for the first 25 years) over 90 degrees to:

- 2014: 21 days;
- 2015: 30 days;
- 2016: 37 days and 72 consecutive frost-free days
- 2017: 51 days and 122 consecutive frosts- free days
- 2018: 67 days and 85 consecutive frost free days

There's global warming up here, no question about it! To boggle the mind, our average frost free days per season is usually between forty seven and fifty! Over the last three years were now averaging about 90!! Almost double, very scary. If this pattern continues my twenty seven shades of greens are going to be in trouble and might have to give way to warm season crops. I definitely will be farming in uncontrolled chaos!

All farmers today are feeling the pressure of climate change across the globe, whether you believe it or not it is happening. Farmers in the near future will feel the impacts on the crops they raise. What crops they grew for decades will no longer be able to be raised because of the changes in temperatures. The changes in weather are becoming more extreme and more frequent. We cannot grow spinach anymore with regularity because our summer soil temperatures are increasing. We are becoming more of the Great Basin high desert community rather than the cooler Sierra Nevada Mountain range.

As the years went by here on the farm it seemed like one-step forward two steps back. I could never get ahead. There was chaos everywhere I turned, not only in the weather. I was winning a few battles, but losing the war, a financial chaos. There was a common denominator, too much money going out, not enough coming in. Bills, bills, bills, they're always on time but my payments were always late or not at all. We were in deep shit, our finances were in disarray, total chaos within the family unit. We had exhausted our credit cards, and maxed out our home equity lines of credit. Kim had had enough and in an uproar. She had spent seventeen years on the farm and helped create Sierra Valley Farms and she saw we were in a dangerous state of going under, and she was right. Kim coming from a white-collar family, her parents had a weekly 9-5 job with weekends off, she had never been exposed to the farming lifestyle we had of not having a weekly paycheck, and having to make your money off the land no matter how long it takes, you keep working and planting more crops to bring in more money. That's how I was taught by dad and his dad and I wasn't going to let this farm fail because it would be a disgrace to my family's generations of farming and ranching. Joey was starting High School and one day after the tensions in our relationship had been high for months, after a lengthy discussion and a peaceful argument, Kim said;

"This is your dream, not mine", and it finally hit home that she needed to pursue her dreams and I was done "dragging her through the mud", I must go on my own to save the farm. Would it be "suicide with a butter knife?" A slow death of the farm, eventually going down with the ship, I don't know but I had to try alone. We split up and since have divorced but have stayed really good friends till this day. I had given Kim the "offering of the olive branch", a peaceful exit from the chaotic farming lifestyle.

We were like most small farmers, we had the financing to start the farm, but as these chaotic situations came about we didn't have the finances to overcome them. Banks discontinued collateral loans, federal loans dried up and crop insurance became too expensive. We relied on credit cards, "robbing Peter-to-pay Paul" and stretching ourselves to thin. We couldn't get off the farm jobs in these rural communities because the wages were too low and we would have to put Joey in daycare so we weren't gaining anything financially. You plug along and it stresses your family life and your motivation to continue to keep farming. This is where many small farmers throw in the towel and say "there has to be a better way." Without any breaks it's hard for a small farm to sustain itself. All small farms need that "one break" to set them free.

So far going into 2019, Sierra Valley Farms has survived the "controlled chaos " environment, and so far we've gotten "that one-break", more like a few little breaks along the way, to get us over the hump. So far, I'm still one of the lucky ones (keep that four-leaf clover under my pillow!) with help from my friends, family, new ventures and a whole lot of luck I'm staying afloat. I always said that a farm can survive and sustain itself if it can stick around long enough. Sooner or later fate will come your way but that's the problem most small farms can't hang around long enough today.

It doesn't really matter what generation of farmer you come from, all of them only had 24 hours in a day and there's a lot of chaos that can go wrong, create havoc and turn gray hairs during that 24 hour period. As I look at it, it's all a mind game. It's how you look at life, and your mind set has a lot to do with how you handle chaotic situations on the farm. Most people "go to work every day to get a paycheck from a salary or a pay wage", small farmers don't get any of that so as a farmer you have to dissect that statement and understand how it doesn't apply to farmers.

First is "go to ", well the farmer doesn't go anywhere, usually the farmer lives where they work, you walk out the front door and you're at work. Second, the farm is 24/7 it never leaves you. You become the farm, the farm is you. Third, the word "work", for the average person is a four-letter word of something you don't want or like to do, it has a negative meaning, the farmer has to look at work as his/her lifestyle, it' our labor of love. For me farming is my way of life. I get up every morning and I farm from morning till night and I know things are going to probably not go as planned so "just deal with it!" Fourth, "get a paycheck from a salary or wage" that's an easy one, farmers don't get a paycheck a salary or a wage (unless you're a subsidized mega farmer that collects what I call their annual agricultural welfare check).

If we added up all our hours working in a day we would be paid pennies per hour. If you want to demoralize and ruin a farmer, the worst thing you can do is have them figure out how much he/she's making an hour and I guarantee they'll quit the first year, and that's what I see colleges doing, they are teaching agriculture to young kids, and especially in small organic farming programs that have in their equation, that a farmer should pay him or herself a living wage, and in reality that's not going to happen for many years in most cases.

Folks, farmers have to look at the big picture, not only the long hours and the hard work, but the financial constraints of low wages, no available loans, no health benefits, or retirement (other than social security) that all creates chaos for the farmer and his/her family. Most beginning farmers can't afford to pay themselves a living wage for the first three years. No wonder there is a 20% decline in the last five years of farmers under forty-five, and why the average age of farmers are my age at 61 and getting older because us old guys have figured that equation out, it's all about the lifestyle, not how much you make an hour! Our retirement for farmers' is the farm, and we either die on it or give it away! Like the joke about when the farmer was asked about winning the lottery:

"What would you do if you win the lottery?

"I will farm until it's all gone!"

I look at my folks and see how successful they were in farming in the Bay Area, San Mateo County, one of the richest and most expensive counties to live, they made it because they never looked at how much they made per hour. They looked at their quality of life (were they doing what they loved to do), and at the end of the year did they have money in their pockets to pay the bills, put some away, and enjoy the things they liked doing. I'd say yes. They weren't extravagant by any means, simple, but lived a good, healthy, Italian lifestyle, relatively chaos free.

I support myself one hundred percent off of farming ventures here on the farm or helping other farmers sell their crops during short periods of down time between my crops. My "controlled chaos" begins in Spring, then to Summer and Fall routines, but summer is the most rigorous and chaotic time of the year with the highest potential of "anything can go wrong at any moment and usually does" here on the farm, juggling plantings, weeding, harvest, attending farmers markets, deliveries to restaurants and natural food stores, family, and putting on my events, this time of year "breeds chaos!".

My day starts as every other; I'm usually up around 5am with a cup of coffee reviewing my "wish list" for that day. It helps not to be a Type "A" personality where everything has to be in perfect order and on time like a Swiss watch, that seldom happens. Mother Nature has her own thoughts on how that day will go and most times you'll have to go along with her, so I go with an open mind knowing that I may have to switch to a plan A, B, or C. On farmers market days I'm out the door loading the truck at 5am and off to a market in the Reno/Tahoe area four days a week then back to the farm by three o'clock to perform my evening chores.

For this particular day its harvest, Chloe (my lab) and I are out the door by 6 am to survey the conditions of my "fields of twenty seven shades of greens" for that day. A lot of the mornings there is a light frost or heavy dew on the greens and we will have to wait an hour or so to let them dry off before harvest. On those days we start harvesting the root crops like carrots, radishes, beets or green onions first. I have my orders made up for the crew on what they are to harvest that day for the Farmers markets and for the restaurants. Years ago hiring a formal crew of laborers and paying wages and workers compensation were killing me. The WWOOF-USA Program (World Wide Opportunity on Organic Farms) didn't work for me because you have to put them up in housing and feed them, and hell I couldn't even keep up with cooking for dad and my son Joey, plus we didn't have housing on the farm for workers, and limited housing in the area. Instead I had a lot of people that I knew from the Farmers markets who said "I'd love to come out to the farm and just pick vegetables for a day, just to get out of the office, or do something different from my real job." So I started a "drop-in" program where you just come out whenever you can and spend about 3-4 hours harvesting vegetables for a combination of vegetables and cash. So every year I attract eight to ten people that come out for a few hours a week to help with the harvest with me, dad and Joey. It's not the most efficient way; in fact it's the most chaotic way to do it. Mainly because you're working with inexperienced people who many have never worked in a garden or even been on a farm, you're just asking for trouble! It takes a little more training and patience from me but it's the most economical way I see it and I enjoy the interaction, and we get it done one chaos or the other.

On this day, Zaya, Erin, and Alejandro show up at 7 am and join me and Joey to begin harvest and I give them their orders and say "The greens are really wet this morning with all the dew, so start with the radishes and carrots, then go to the greens later when they're dry", they say "Ok", and they're off on the golf carts to harvest greens along with Chloe. Dad comes out of the Guest house (where he lives 8 months of the year) across the driveway from my house and Dad says

"What do you want me to do today", so I say

"Take the Kubota with the mower unit and go mow the five acres of pasture for the blues concert we have coming up next weekend. We'll need it mowed for parking cars and our overnight RVs." Dad said

"Do I need diesel?" I said

"No you're good to go!"

So off my 91 year old dad went to mow the field. While the crew was harvesting, and dad was mowing, I had to get on hand weeding the next crop of greens, because my weekend crew of immigrant workers didn't show up for the last two weekends because now that "dipshit #45" is president the Mexicans don't want to take a chance of being deported so they are not traveling to these rural areas for work, which has caused chaos on my weed program, so I have to do it. After about an hour I hear the Kubota shut off at the far end of the pasture and I can see dad looking under the mower and I knew right away he caught something in the rotating blades. So plan B, leave the hand weeding to go see what kind of trouble dad's in. As I got closer I could hear him swearing in Italian, that "the wire shouldn't have been there", that it wasn't his fault even though when he turned, the mower unit went into the fence (Italian logic), he just went too close to the fence in the first place and the rotating blades caught the wire and wrapped it around the main shaft. This is a major project. So back to the shop and I spend an hour cutting and unwinding this barbed wire from the shaft of the mower, while dad goes to the Veterans Hall for lunch. I then go back to my hand weeding. After lunch I see the crew carrying the fifteen gallon bags of greens to the packing sheds so I say to Joey.

"Hey guys, how did it go this morning", and as 18 year old kids do... Joey says

"Ah...ok, I guess", but when I look in the bags of greens they're total soaked from the morning dew, I was in an uproar,

"Damn it Joey I told you guys to let the greens dry first", he rolls his eyes and everyone kind of disappears in the packing shed, and I say

"Well you and Alejandro are going to have to dry them somehow", (another plan B).

We didn't have a salad spinner big enough to spin about 100 pounds of greens so I said to the boys "Let's do this...take the greens in the house, put them loosely in the washing machine, and put it on the spin cycle, it runs for about five minutes, take them out then do another batch (I had done that before and it worked great, especially for coarser leafy greens like spinach and arugula)." So back to weeding I went, figuring the boys would have it under control... (NOT) and something didn't sound right, the sound I heard was not the washer running but the dryer...No Fucking way! I ran and screamed at Joey,

"What the fuck are you doing? I told you the spin cycle in the washer, not the dryer!!!" I laugh now but at the time I could have killed him. Luckily I caught it on the first bag of spring mix, and as I opened the dryer door they were "mush", like creamed spinach...Yuk!

Joey said:

"I just thought they would dry faster"

I said:

"You are Italian", now clean up the mess in the dryer and finish the rest on the spin cycle, and they did it right and finished bagging the greens and putting up the orders for the rest of the day. This day was total "uncontrolled chaos" on the farm!

By now it was about 2 pm and over 95 degrees and I only got about an hour worth of weeding done out of the last five hours so I had a lot of catching up to do. So I grabbed a canteen of water and I continued on my hands and knees pulling weeds in the hot sun until about 6 pm in which my fingers were numb from weeding, parched by the sun, and I was looking cross-eyed from having my face so close to the ground. My knees we frozen into this crouched position and as I stood up I felt stiff as a board and glued to the ground, like trying to peel off a piece of scotch tape from a box. As I got up I stood there a few minutes, then stretched a few minutes to get my circulation back to my fingers and limbs…then I whispered to myself in a sigh…"I'm getting too old for this shit", as I went in to make dinner. After putting in a load of wash and finishing the dishes my day wasn't over yet. I had to go out and check the three hoop houses to see if the sweet peppers and the tomatoes needed evening water. So I grabbed my tall gin and tonic and checked the peppers and tomatoes and gave them a shot of water, now it was time to go turn on the drip systems for all the greens, two acres in all so far at the time of the season, turning on four different valves that evening so that the lettuces wouldn't wilt after that hot summer day. Of course when I turned the valves on the voles (meadow mice) had chewed a few holes in each of the different drip lines of each valve so I had to spend about another hour repairing the holes before irrigating. I was on my last valve about 8:30 pm. The rest were repaired and shut down. I had to leave this last valve on for another hour to get a good soak on the spring mixes before I shut them off, so I went inside to have another cocktail and relax and watch my San Francisco Giants. The last thing I remember was waking up in my Lazy Boy recliner at 1:30am and thinking "Shit I pulled another Romano",(as I have named it when I forget to shut off a water valve and leave it on too long.), so on this full moon early morning, I'm running out in my "skivvies" to shut off the water. I'm sure it wasn't a pretty sight! The final step in a chaotic day!

When you farm year round, especially in these harsh mountain conditions, farming in chaos is inevitable. No matter how well you plan, "shit happens" and you have to be ready for it and control it, because it can quickly become pandemonium. As you can see farming is a lot of work, long hours, a labor of love, without much monetary reward, and still farming at 61. I still love it, wouldn't want to do anything else but farm. As I get older I'm getting tired though, and being by myself with a little help from my friends and drop-ins it starts to wear on you, I get frustrated when I see things falling between the cracks because I can't keep up with the workload and that "controlled chaos" that you used to "control" starts slipping away. The farm is aging as I am and I can see some decline and I wonder how long I can continue at this pace at my age. When I bought the farm in 1989 I was full of "spit and vinegar" and it looked like fun and I could "control" all the chaos, and now that I'm getting older it's not always "fun and games anymore." That's just the life of a farmer. It sounds glamorous and people think farmers are immortal and go on farming forever, but in reality the hard work and the farm wear on an aging farmer.

As the age of the American Farmer gets older every year now around the age of 62, these older farmers are having a hard time keeping up their farms. The kids have moved off the farms to desk jobs in the city, and with labor costs rising, the aging farmer can't afford to pay for labor or because of the deportation of immigrants, they can't even get the illegal ones anymore so their farms start falling apart. They can't work as hard as they used to, health problems arise and lack of motivation sets in. Many just walk off the farm and others go to the extreme of suicide. It's becoming a real problem because the younger generations don't want to farm, there's no money in it, and if they want to they can't afford to. We will have a real farming crisis in America in the next fifteen years. We will need hundreds of thousands of new farmers, and where will they come from with no incentives to farm let along we're now three plus generations away from people having the knowledge and experience of knowing how to farm once us old timers are gone.

As I get older, and being on my own, my feelings relate to Peter Dunning's quote...(Documentary: Peter and the Farm) *it's all I ever wanted and I alone can't do it. I watch the sills rot, the fields get taken over by weeds, the fences falling down, the barn leans, each building* fills with crap, and dirt, decay, and clutter, the house peels and sag, where in the fuck can I go. My life has been spent improving this farm. Never have the fields flourished, I have succeeded, the diversity of wildlife, richness, the beauty. It only cost me two children and two wives, but I kept the farm. But this man is slowing down and the weeds are speeding up. But what else? Where else?

We all have to face reality, but the fact is that farmers are a dying breed. We are the Farmasaur, and not many of us are around anymore. How many more years of productivity do I have in me, or want to farm at this level? Can I handle all the "controlled" and "uncontrolled" chaos that happens on a daily basis? Farmers are like everyone else as we get older we all must deal with the fact that we're going be gone someday. I told Joey the other day, I said" You should know what to do with this farm when I'm gone, because you're the next in line." I told him the details of the legal and financial situations of the farm and I said "You never know you're future you could end up like me running away from farming, but missing all the chaos, then coming back to the farm. The farm is finally paid off and in a trust for you so when I'm gone you can do what you wish, the good news is it' in a conservation easement with the Land Trust to be an organic farm for eternity, it can never be developed and only kept as an organic farm, the bad news is you won't get as much money for it if you sell it!"

"As for me…just sprinkle my ashes over the pond by the tiki bar (there is a pond and tiki bar I built at the east end of the farm) because… *there's not a part of this farm that has not been scattered with my spit, my shit, my sweat, my piss, my skin, my blood, my seed, fingernails, skin or hair.* (Quote from Peter Dunnings documentary *Peter and the Farm*) …so if I have to go to "greener pastures" I'd rather be scattered in the pond and maybe for once there will be no chaos, the olive branch of peace has been given to me at last.

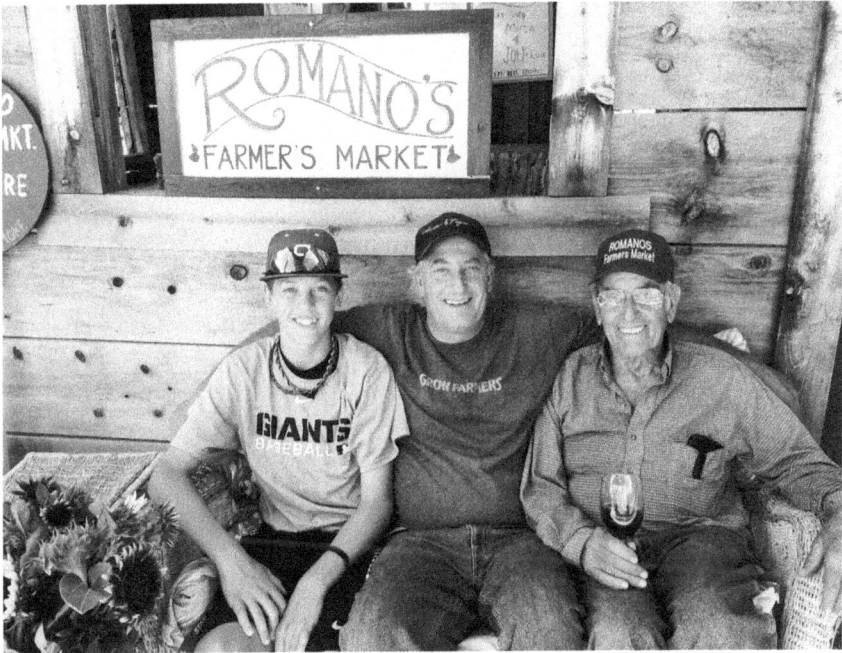

Three generations of Romano's: Joey, Gary, and Lou.

Shamrock Green

A Little Help from My Friends

*"Green is the prime color of the world and
that from which its loveliness arises."*
Pedro Calderon de la Barca

I've selected the color shamrock green to represent this chapter because I've been lucky to get a lot of help from my friends over the years to sustain my farm. As a farmer I distinguish my friends in many forms, my human and animal friends as inner-skeletal (their skeletons or on the inside) and my exoskeleton (their skeletons are on the outside) those friends are my insect friends; and combined this small organic farmer gets a lot of help from all of my friends!

The shamrock is associated with good luck and fortune in the Irish culture and tradition (Even though I'm Italian I feel lucky and fortunate to be able to continue farming as a third generation farmer). The green color of the shamrock is considered lucky because of its abundance and prevalence in nature. Its three green petals represent the balancing of forces in a multitude of ways. This connection to abundance and joyful, healthy prosperity was a good omen for the Irish farmers who wanted their livestock to be well fed. The fragrance of the shamrock's green leaf has a calming effect on the body and mind allowing a person to relax and feel content. That is the feeling of this aging organic farmer.

In order for small farmers to survive in the 21st Century we will need not only the luck of the shamrock, but also a lot of help from our friends, community, and our policy makers in order to save the small family farmer from extinction. Land will need to become affordable for young farmers. Farmers must be treated as a non-profit (we currently make less than poverty wages so we might as well be), tax exempt and eligible for zero interest and collateral loans along with new markets to help distribute our goods into our local communities. Every farmer I know needs help on the farm sometime or another, and whether you admit it or not, you can't do it all yourself and know it all. Some think they do, but I'm the first one to admit that I know a little about a lot of things but not a lot on a few things. Coming from the Beatles, Sargent Pepper's Lonely Hearts Club Band Album the song "With a Little Help from My Friends", how true it is on my farm, I couldn't have got things done without friends of all forms.

Throughout the book I will be talking about people who have in-fluenced my life and been a part of the farm, for their privacy I will only be using their first name or nickname and the stories I tell are all in good humor. In the end, I love them all and all have chapters that tell the story of Sierra Valley Farms, and if you want to read more stories about life on the farm pick up a copy of my *Why I Farm: Risking it all for a Life on the Land.*

As the saying goes "You got to know people in the right places", how true it is, because when you start out as a new farmer, you're green, young and energetic, with tons of ideas on what you're going to do on your new farm, but most times you have more time than money. You need a little luck to go your way. That's my story. This farm needed a lot of work when I bought it and trying to transform an eighty year old livestock ranch into a progressive native plant nursery and organic vegetable farm I was going to need more than a little help from my friends, I needed to know the people in the right places to get things done, and I was lucky to have friends in the right places to pull from to get me started.

Basically, most farmers are a "Jack of all trades, and master of none", and that's me as well. To be a farmer you have to not only know how to farm or grow things, but be a plumber, mechanic, electrician, carpenter, roofer, mason, veterinarian, welder-fabricator, horticulturist, entomologist, soil scientist, counselor, foreman, land manager, equipment operator, salesman, computer geek, bookkeeper, boss, and husband/wife (optional). About twenty-shades of a farmer, my true colors The key is to find these trades amongst your existing family and get a little help from your friends, or" find - a-friend-of-a-friend-of-a-friend... until you've exhausted all channels and then you have to pay through the nose for a professional."

Rob was my old roommate from college in Chico, when I went back for my Master's Degree in 1985. We had met through a friend years before when I was at Cal Poly San Luis Obispo getting my undergraduate degree in Parks & Recreation after I left the flower farm. (I was finally done with farming...NOT!). We partied so much down at Cal Poly that Rob decided to transfer to Chico State to "dry out" (Chico State was the #1 party school in the nation at that time), and we met up again years later. In 1991 Rob a general contractor was out of work and I had a lot of projects to get done here on the farm, the main one was to construct three greenhouse kits that I had purchased and repair and transform a lot of the old shacks into useable nursery and farm buildings. So I called Rob and said "Hey Rob, Can you come up here and build these greenhouses for me?" Rob being joke full as he was said "How much are you going to pay me?" I said "I'll take care of you...the checks in the mail!" It was a go, Rob moved up to the farm in the summer of 1991. He worked diligently through the summer to build these greenhouses and transform these shacks around here into usable buildings. These greenhouse kits were pallets of nuts and bolts like a huge erector set. Rob battled the summer wind storms, thunder storms, and the heat of those summer days and was amazing on how he figured them out. On the day of truth, when all was in place, we loaded all eight of the trusses on the top of my old '66 dump truck; it was just the right height to back in and slide the trusses onto the posts. The posts had to be just perfect in order for the prefabricated trusses to fit right onto the posts. It was incredible, each truss fit perfectly! It was "beer-thirty", time to PARTY!!! We closed up the end wall and it was off to the Beckwith Tavern to celebrate! To my surprise, the next morning while I was at my parks office in Truckee (My final days working for Truckee Parks and Recreation), I get a call from Rob.

"Hey, have you seen the dump truck?"

"No, we used it last in the greenhouse," I said.

A moment of silence passed between us.

"Oh shit, did we close it in the greenhouse last night?"

Yes, we did. Through all the excitement (and maybe a few beers), we had closed the end of the greenhouse, forgetting that the dump truck was inside—now that's Italian! Rob then had to cut out the end wall out and we drove it out and closed it back in, but it all turned out awesome, that was a lot of help from my friend Rob.

Throughout those first years in the 1990's a lot of my close friends came up for weekends and would work for barbeques and beers. They were all from the Bay Area and just wanted to come up and hang out at the farm, shoot guns, ride ATV's and do a little work. My buddy Tony and would come over from Reno and we would jack up some of the old shacks, brace them up and put logs under them, hook them to a couple of tractors I had and drag them to wherever I needed them. Some made it intact, others fell apart along the way and I'd push them into a pile and burn them or salvage the old barn wood.

Ray and Wendy was a young couple in their twenties, from Chilcoot, Wendy was pregnant and Ray was in and out of jobs, and this particular week out of work. Ray was a young, quit witted, loud guy with a crazy look in his eyes, but always joking around having fun. We had just started our farm stand selling fruits and vegetables from other growers as well as our organic greens, this was around 2005, and Wendy and Ray were our best customers. Ray came up to me that day and said

"Gary, do you have any need for an excavator?" I said

"Why?"

"Well I'm out of work, and my dad has an excavation business in Reno, and I can bring a D8 Caterpillar out and grade anything you want for this month's rent of $500.00", Ray said.

Looking at Wendy pregnant, I thought, "I need to find a project to help this young couple out", so I had this dream all along about having a pond on the farm with and island in the middle, a moat around it with a Tiki Bar dead center in the middle of the island.

I knew that to do this project on my own would cost tens of thousands of dollars so I said, "Ray, yes I do", and I told him about the project, that the Sierra Valley sloughs used to come into the northeast corner of my property and when my neighbor damned off the slough going to my property I lost the water. The depression was still evident. Also I was fighting a neighboring rock quarry about a proposed asphalt batch plant that they were proposing and the drainage from the upper quarry crosses my fields to the sloughs below me. I wanted to have him cut a drainage ditch from the south corner of my fields that would capture the run off from the quarry and divert it around my fields to the pond. Ray was then going to install an old culvert I had and create a spillway. The thought was as the run off enters the pond the toxins would settle out and when the pond rose to the spillway the cleaner water on top would then exit the spillway into the sloughs which feed the headwaters of the Middle Fork of the Feather River a mile downstream, to protect the ecosystem.

Ray said

"No problem...we build ponds all the time and that's my dad's specialty, I've done it before... "I'll be here Saturday morning at 8 am!"

That Saturday Ray and his dad off-loaded the D8 and Ray spent all week cutting and grading, using his land level he was focused on the end result, my pond and Tiki bar which I already called *"Lago Romano."* He finished the project on the following Sunday, and was finishing the final touches on the grading of the pond, it was late September and he left the D8 at the bottom of the pond which was about 12 feet deep and about a half an acre.

Ray said

"Dad and I will come pick it up (D8) in the morning." I said

"Ok…this looks great!"

Ray had done everything I had asked him and then some and I gave him an extra one hundred dollars, $600 total and happy to do so. The next morning I was out in the fields harvesting greens about 7 am and I hear Ray screaming at the top of his lungs "Water, Water, Fucking Water!", as he was jumping jubilantly on top of the roll bar cage of the D8. He had hit the ground water table and overnight it began to fill the pond. As I ran to greet Ray, I could see the D8 was sitting in about three feet of water. Ray did a few other small grading projects the following week for the next month's rent.

For the record I did get a Plumas County and a California Water Resources permit for the pond during the construction The last I saw of Ray was at our farm stand a couple of weeks later and he came up to me and said,

" Hey…these are for Joey,… these (small cast iron) John Deere toy tractors were mine when I was Joeys age…man…thanks for the work you saved us",

Joey was about four and played with those for years and I still have them on display at our Farmers Market today. Years later I heard Ray and Wendy divorced and Wendy re-married, and no one really knows where Ray is today.

Other influential friends that helped me on the farm over the years are:, My buddy Mark is my electrician guy and loves to talk "won't shut-up" and loves go to the Reno Farmers Market with my dad "Lou", and is my dog sitter for Chloe when I have to leave town: Rick is my local mechanic, he can fix anything. He owned a garage in Incline Village and is retired: Bob is my local retired carpenter who loves to just get away from town and take Chloe for a walk looking for arrow heads, he is my "handy man" helping me with small construction projects around the farm and keeps me well fed with trout from the surrounding lakes (he doesn't like fish): and Rand builds incredible wood crafted canoes and over the years has helped me remodel the guest cottage that dad lives in and built my so important Tiki Bar on the pond.

The beauty of being a small farmer is the lifestyle. You are your own boss, you don't punch a clock 9-5 and have to be somewhere at a particular time, and your day is never dull. Your priorities change hourly depending on what needs to be done on that particular day and what resources you have to pull from amongst your community and family of friends.

About fifteen years ago after we built all the green houses, we had a huge wind storm that thrashed the old pig shed was ready to fall down and I didn't have a use for it, I just wanted to plant my vegetables in that space to utilize the fifty years of "pig shit" that was there. My veterinarian Martin, was the fire chief of the volunteer Beckwourth Fire Department, so I called him and said

"Martin, do you want to put on a training session for your volunteer fireman and burn down the rest of my pig shed?"

He said

"Awesome let's do it!"

A couple weekends later he called and was ready to do it. They showed up with sirens blaring and lights flashing, the whole department of six guys. They prepped and got all their gear ready. The pig shed was pretty good size, about the size of a small house, so when they were ready they "set it ablaze." It was a tinder box, went up immediately. I looked at Martin and him and his crew were laughing, and pulling all these small propane tanks out of their back packs and

I said

"What are you going to do with those?"

Martin said

"Watch"

As he and is fireman buddies started throwing these propane canisters into the blaze.

Martin said

"Stand back you never know where these things go when they explode"

They began "hissing and pissing" and we all ran for it as they started to explode and shot about fifty feet in the air. These guys were "Pyro's"; I guess that's why they're fireman. They then put out the fire, and did the cleanup. In all, it was a good training session, but "boys will be boys", they made it fun.

A few years later, Martin was a big "civil war nut" and he had a small civil war cannon that he would fire off every new year's, well this one year I could hear the cannon go off at new year's, and I didn't pay much attention I knew it was Martin. About a month later I was cleaning up around the back of my greenhouse and about a fifty yards away I saw what I thought was one of Joey' kick balls, I figured the wind had blown it out in the field, when I went to pick it up it was a bowling ball. I thought about it for a few minutes and said to myself "How it the hell did a bowling ball get out here?" I looked up in the sky, did it fall out of a plane "what the hell", then the light went on and I said "God damn Martin, he's been shooting bowling balls out of the cannon, and shit, this one could have gone through my greenhouse of even my house!" So I went in the house and called him, he answered the phone and

I said

"Martin, are you missing a bowling ball?"

There was a little silence then

He replied

"No way

I said

"Yes way...it landed by my greenhouse!

He said

"I'm sorry we shot them towards the middle of Sierra Valley, how did they get there?"

Well the finger holes of the bowling ball must have made it curve like a curve ball.

Martin said"

Just don't tell my wife!"

We laughed and I gave him back his bowling ball but every New Year's Eve I don't sleep very well!

In general, all types of people are attracted to Farms; it sounds glamorous, kind of mystic, "What actually goes on at a farm?" People are intrigued with farms and farmers, they have no clue how their food is raised or any idea of how much work it is to put food on the public's table. Most people today never have access to any farms; they just see them on their travels along the highways and catch a quick glimpse of them flying by sixty five miles an hour. The people that look for work on farms, at least that have come to my farm, are young, mostly women, usually liberal, free-in spirit, kind of nomads that have no roots, transient in nature and well educated but pretty much greenhorns when it comes to actually farming and not looking for full time work, like the shamrock these people have a connection to the abundance within a farm and they have a joyful spirit for a healthy future. They have a "let me work for a while and see if I like it" attitude and when the season is over and they continue their travels and can say "yea, I worked on an organic farm in the mountains it was pretty cool!" This group of individuals I really enjoy they have been the back bone of Sierra Valley Farms, harvesting most of my summer vegetables for the past fifteen years. Every Spring I reach out to the ones that have worked for me in previous years to see if they want to come back, and

I'm always contacted by "newbies" looking for a few hours a week. As I said earlier, I try to get a pool of six to eight people that I can pull from that want to work a few hours per week for a combination of produce and cash. I have to stay under the California State Law of not paying over $600 per person so the more people I have working less hours keeps me safe. For my other "drop-ins", they have real jobs and this is spending money, or travel money for them.

Every once in a while and if you're lucky enough to find these shamrocks, a person who comes along that really creates an impact on your life and the farm. Every farmer hopefully can find one or two people that become a vital part of their operation. I'd say Larry and Ryan; you know who you were an influential part of the farm and to our immediate family and why I'm still lucky enough to be farming after all these years.

Larry was an integral part of helping me go to organic vegetables during the early years of Sierra Valley Farms. At the time from 2002-2005 I was growing a lot of native plants for government projects and Larry and I were doing a lot of transplanting and seeding of native plants, but we were losing our ass and had to transform the nursery operation to organic vegetables. Larry was here all the time. Joey was small and took most of Kim's time so she couldn't help much on the farm so I depended on Larry. He was definitely my "right-hand man." Larry was from British Columbia, and would arrive in late April with his trailer and work until October; he would then go down to the Central Coast of California for the winter landscaping and making lip balms and salves from the flowers of St. John's Wort that he collected in the wilds of the surrounding Sierra mountains in September. Larry was a great guy, mellow, slim build, longish brown/gray, was transient-- kind of a nomad, always broke, a reformed drug-user, smoked a little weed, liked his wine, he would set up his trailer behind the barn and we would sit out by the meadow after a long day's work and sip wine and have a hit-or-two of his "ganja" and watch the sunset. When Joey was little about five or six years old Joey would like to go over to his trailer and ask Larry a bunch of questions, Joey liked the smell of his "sage-incense" that was always smoldering and leaving a light fog inside his trailer. After the season of 2006, in October Larry introduced me to his son from British Columbia and they worked together landscaping and I never saw Larry after that, I did here he is still down in the Central Coast. Love you Larry hope you're enjoying life!

I consider all the people (drop-ins) that have worked on my farm as special friends, part of the family and thank them so much for supporting Sierra Valley Farms, and I welcome them all back. I'll probably miss a few names and I apologize, but here the ones that have harvested my twenty seven shades of green and I thank you: Larry, Ryan, Randy, Megan, Anna, Bob, Lauren, Zaya, Rand, Amy 1; Amy 2, Amy 3, Mary, Beenie, Erin, Alejandro, Grace, Destiny, Zoey, Samantha, Cody, Katie, Elizabeth, Corin, Justin, Tammy, Traci, Sam, Jon(and buddies), Camilla, Heather, Greg, Annie and I'm sure I'm missing a few in the early years.

In the summer of 2011 after a heavy snow year, I was late getting my greens in and found myself scrambling to put a crew together for the season. One morning the phone rang and as I answered it I heard

"Hey Gary...Its Ryan...you know I was the sous chef at Moody's in Truckee, I said

"Oh yea, what happened to you I haven't seen you there anymore, Ryan said

"Gary... man...I went up to help Mark Estee start another restaurant, Baxters at Northstar...dude...then I went off the road and hit a tree and totaled my car...man... and I couldn't get to work so they laid me off...dude... I live in Sierraville (about 18 miles away) now and wondered if you need any help?" I said

"Matter of fact yea, but how are you going to get here?"

He said "I'll ride my bike,

"It's about 18 miles one way" I replied.

"That's ok" he said

"Ok, I'll see you tomorrow morning, be here at seven"

As I hung up the phone, I remembered Ryan in the kitchen at Moody's Bistro and Lounge, he was blonde, tall, a skier, very athletic, scrappy looking, very intense, but always working really hard, loud, and if you ask him a question he didn't mind "telling it like it is." He was in his early thirties and was from Pennsylvania and did his culinary work for Armani in Italy and for prominent chefs in New York and Boston before landing in Lake Tahoe and Truckee. I remember Ryan was an amazing chef, Michael Plapp the Executive chef at Baxters would talk about his talents as a chef. Ryan wasn't outgoing or social, he didn't like to be amongst crowds, he was kind of a loner.

Ryan showed up the next morning right on time, and we hit it off very well catching up on old times from when he worked at Moody's. Ryan was done with being a chef. He said he was tired of the "late night life, partying after hours which lead him to drugs, alcohol and un healthy lifestyle. He wanted to learn how to farm and someday have his own organic farm which included livestock. Ryan was very knowledgeable about organic food, organic farming and biodynamic farming. He had never worked on a farm before and was a total green-horn, and he admitted it, but was eager to learn as much as he could about farming. He became a "sponge" around me soaking up as much information about organic farming practices as possible and asking a million questions. He considered me the "guru of organic greens" in the Reno/Tahoe area, and spoke highly of me to the other chefs, while working in Tahoe. He was well aware of Sierra Valley Farms.

Ryan was a diabetic, Type 1, I believe, and the day he totaled his car his blood insulin levels were out of whack and he passed out at the wheel, and running into a tree outside of Truckee, luckily not seriously hurt, but he lost his driver's license due to his medical condition. Ryan was a very energetic person and one of the hardest working people I've ever had on the farm, but he was like herding cats, going in multiple directions without a focus. I would have to constantly check on him to keep him focused on the task at hand. He definitely was the entertainment for Tammy, Panna, Amy and Grace who worked alongside Ryan that season. They kept him in check while he chewed their ears off about the philosophy of life, organic food, biodynamic farming and livestock. Over the course of the season, the girls would pick him up on the way to the farm or I would go get him, and I helped him get his health back in shape and he was able to get his driver's license back by the end of 2011.Ryan worked two more seasons here on the farm and was pretty much part of the family unit with Kim, Joey and I. We had just got Chloe, our English black lab as a puppy in 2011 and Ryan would bring his dog Ruby a mixed lab to play with her. Ruby actually would go down to the pond (where the tiki bar is) to swim and Chloe would follow her and Ruby actually taught her how to swim (got her to go in the water). They became the best of friends!

By 2013 Ryan was a seasoned veteran here on the farm and knew most of the farming techniques and the equipment here on the farm. We were a machine together, Amy and Grace were still working here and it was fun times, we got a lot of work done. At the end of the season I was planning on attending the Eco Farm Conference at Asilomar in Pacific Grove, California, near Monterey. As a surprise to me, Ryan offered to pay for mine and his registration to the conference in January for all the help I had given him getting his life back together. We planned the trip which was about a five to six hour drive from the farm. You have to understand Ryan first, he was very intense in a way that he seemed to always be the cart ahead of the horse, kind of scattered most times "like a chicken with his head cut off" and hard on equipment, just because he didn't have a lot of experience around tractors, or small farm equipment. With this thought in mind, we left on this January day for the Conference in Monterey. Ryan was going to drive to Sacramento, and then I was going to take over and drive the rest of the way. We got to Sacramento and changed drivers and I took over the reins. Along the drive Ryan and I talked about everything and anything about organic vs. biodynamic farming, livestock, food, crops etc. about the time we get to San Ramon on highway 80, I was starting to merge to the second lane to prepare to get onto highway 580 towards San Francisco when I felt a huge vibration in the vehicle and it immediately turned into a violent shaking and suddenly the vehicles back end dropped to the ground with a loud screeching noise, as I see this tire go flying in front of us bouncing 30 feet in the air about 80 miles an hour, hitting the concrete abutment then rolling to a stop and luckily out of traffic. Our rear passenger tire had sheared off the hub and literally passed us up, luckily I was able to control the vehicle and skid off the road safely. When I came to a stop, white knuckles and all I looked at Ryan and said "Shit" he and I began laughing hysterically, and as only Ryan can express the situation he said "Gaar...WTF just happened? We got out, retrieved the tire, and what had happened was Ryan had gotten a flat tire a few days before and changed that tire but evidently he either didn't tighten the lug nuts, or the tire was put on in a way that the rim wasn't even with the hub and over the long drive the "wobbling" of the tire sheared all the lug nuts right off. Luckily we didn't get hurt, but like I said Ryan was good at a lot of things but equipment wasn't his strong point. Luckily my buddy Mark lived a few miles away and we towed Ryan's car to a Big "O" tire shop to be repaired, Mark took us to mom and dads about 45 minutes in away in Redwood City to borrow one of dad's trucks. Ryan and I then went to the conference for two days and spent the evenings talking to other farmers and staying up late discussing the sessions we attended drinking a lot of wine and homemade grappa. Ryan had found his direction in life, to become a farmer.

Ryan left the farm in 2014 and took a job at a biodynamic winery, Hirsch Winery above the Russian River doing biodynamic preparations for the vineyard. In October of 2017, Ryan came to visit it me here on the farm excited to tell me that he just bought a 40 acre farm in New York. He spent the night here and we drank wine and homemade grappa just like old times and got caught up on our lives and the potential of his new farm. Chloe was so glad to see him she never left his side, but Ruby his Labrador, had to be left in New York because her hips were failing as she was over twelve years old now. Ryan had just bought a newer Toyota Tacoma and my son Joey had just left for college and left an extra set of snow tires from his Toyota Tacoma that he didn't want, so the next morning I said to Ryan

"Hey... here's a gift for you, take these four snow tires, you'll need them this winter in New York, but this time have a tire shop put them on!"

We laughed and as he drove away

I said

"Good luck buddy, you did it... You got your farm! I'll come and visit.

Farm animals weren't considered "friends" for me when I bought the farm because when I was a kid watching the uncles fed, water, nourish milk and slaughter them, was a big commitment. One that I didn't want to deal with, but dogs and cats are different. A farmer's got to have a farm dog and barn cats. These are my "fuzzy" friends of the farm.

Dogs are a farmers' best friend! Every farmer must have a dog(s). Dogs are great because they are not only our protectors, but they pick up our spirits after a long day. They always love you no matter how shitty your day was or how much chaos you had to deal with that day. They just wag their tail and say "pet me, feed me, lets' go play!"

When I got the farm going in 1991 I had just got married to my first wife Tami, a registered nurse working in Reno, and we had our wonderful daughter Elizabeth. When I married Tami she came with "doggie baggage", Joskey and Justin, two small to medium "muts" (mixture of many breeds), they were soon joined by Bo, and a long haired mixed Labrador that was given to us from one of Tami's friends. They all were a joy on the farm, Justin, the smallest was a shaggy, cute

Pomeranian-type dog that stayed in the house at night, while Joskey (who looked like a cross of a Dingo and Coyote), short-haired and very fast, and Bo would stay out at night they didn't like the house. Sometimes Joskey would stay in when Tami was home. Bo was a crazy lab, he didn't mind the cold. One morning I went out to let him in and it had snowed a couple inches and Bo was laying on the lawn covered in snow, I was afraid he froze to death, as I opened up the door, he jumped up, half of him was white as snow, the other was black, I wish I had my cell phone then to take his selfie! Bo had incredible endurance, I would fly across the meadow with my ATV in fourth gear and he would stay toe-to- toe with me for over a mile. I've never seen a dog like him, in the mornings when I would let him in to feed him he would be all covered in sticks from the sage brush, all dusty and dirty from running all night. Tami and I assumed he would run with the coyotes, or from the coyotes, he was never chewed up though, I wasn't worried about him he was healthy and happy, plus there was no way a coyote was going to out run him.

Years later after Tami and I divorced and she left with Elizabeth and Justin (the small house dog), I was alone here on the farm with Joskey and Bo and commuting to my Parks and Recreation job in Truckee and I didn't have a kennel to keep Bo and Joskey in, so I left them to roam. I think Bo liked to chase cars or anything that moved, and Joskey would just follow him. On this one sad Easter day, I went to let the dogs in and they weren't at the door, they were always at the door…I went looking for them and found Joskey dead by the barn and Bo barely alive by the bunk house; they had been poisoned by rat poison. I called my buddy Martin the veterinarian, and rushed Bo over to try a blood transfusion from another dog but he died on the operating table. I'm guessing, but someone must have been upset with the two dogs chasing cars or whatever they were chasing and threw out meat with rat poison in it. Ranchers around here are known to do that. I was crushed and swore never to get another dog again until 2011 when Joey and Kim convinced me to get Chloe and after six years (Kim has left and Joey is off to college) now again it's just the farmer and his best friend.

All farms must have barn cats, my other "fuzzy" friends. There are two kinds of cats: house cats and barn cats. Cats can't be both to survive Sierra Valley. House cats are true greenhorns to the "wild west" of the mountains, the wild frontier. They are naïve to the cruel world of "survival of the fittest." They normally won't survive a night against, coyotes, eagles, owls and any other predators. The one little kitty (Girlie) Joey had as a kid was a house cat that got carried off by a great-horned owl the first night we let her out. But feral barn cats are different. They are "street-smart", or as I say "Farm smart", they learn quickly about the dangers that face the farm –predators.

There is a long-haired breed of feral cat that has been around for generations here in Sierra Valley, and I don't know the breed, a mid-size cat with tons of fur to handle the harsh winters. They look like mini musk ox running across the frozen tundra during the winter, and during the summer they shed huge "clumps" of fur to handle to hot temperatures. Twenty years ago, when Kim was pregnant with Joey, someone dumped four kittens on our driveway. I cut a hole in the foundation of the bunkhouse and they've been living under there since. We named them Kato (orange color), Foxy (beautiful gray-brown) and Pepper (black color) and "Pretty Pup" (Joey named him at three years old, a long-haired tabby), these cats were amazing, they would catch weasels, jack rabbits, squirrels, brush cottontails, voles, mice you name it. The farm was clean of varmints! Kato, the orange cat was the last to pass away last year at 22 years old.

This one day I was trying to shoot a ground squirrel that was sitting on top of the burn pile with my .22 rifle and I kept missing it, then the next morning as I was walking to the truck, Pretty-Pup was meowing profusely at me my the side of the truck, as I approached the truck I see her proudly displaying her kill, she had killed that ground squirrel I kept missing as to say "See, I guess if you can't kill it, I have to do it!"

Every farm has to have feral cats; they are very independent and keep rodents under control in my hoop house and barns.

Next are my fine "feathered" friends, Birds. Sierra Valley has birds of all kinds' songbirds, game birds, and birds of prey. Plumas Audubon does a winter and summer bird count that is visited by hundreds of bird watchers as they scan Sierra Valley to get a glimpse of our wide variety of bird life. It carries over to our farm as these birds of all kinds not only feast on small insects rodents and small mammals, but bring joy to the farm, "music to our ears" as we listen to the meadow larks sing, the sand hill cranes, crows and magpies squawk, the valley quail chuckle and the flocks of Canadian geese bellow on their migration through Sierra Valley. The one group that are my favorite feathered friends that I'm lucky to have, are the birds of prey, Raptors: Owls, hawks, falcons and eagles. We have them all, and many overwinter here in Sierra Valley, you can see them on every fence post, telephone pole, or high in the cottonwood trees, and circling above this grandiose alpine valley. We have Red-shouldered hawks, Red-tail hawks, Northern Harrier, Rough-legged hawks, Ferruginous hawks, Kites and more. We have the speedy and agile falcons: American kestrel, Peregrine and Prairie Falcons and plenty Owls: Barn Owl, Great-horned owl, Long-eared Owls, Grey owls, and burrowing owls. On to the most popular, Eagles: Winter time we have an abundance of Bald eagles, Golden eagles and the fish eagle, the Osprey. What these raptors don't finish the turkey vultures and ravens do. This group of raptors is vital to controlling rodents and small mammal pests (rabbits, weasels, ground squirrels, voles, gophers, mice) within our farm. We cut openings and provide platforms in our barns and out buildings so that they can roost and create their nests, and many just come in to over winter here on our farm and are gone by late spring. I have a bald eagle we name "baldy" who hangs out for a couple weeks after Christmas on our large cottonwood tree by the house and watches Chloe run around and me do my chores all day long only about 30 feet over our heads. They're just such a majestic bird and I'm honored just to be able to be in his presence. This group of raptors, help control rodents, and many of the song birds, flycatchers, and flocks of black birds, meadow larks, bluebirds, robins and sparrows help to control our insect pests as well and bring a joy of music to the farm.

My last group of friends that are in abundance on this organic farm, are ones you don't think about too much, and largely go unnoticed, these are my exoskeltal friends(insects have their skeletons on the outside to protect their insides): beneficial insects. Like the shamrock they represent the balancing of forces in a multitude of ways in nature. By creating natural habitats for these wonderful insects they in turn give me a lot of help in minimizing pest damage on our crops. I get a lot of help from these friends. So who are my exoskeletal friends? They are: lady bugs, green lace wings, dragon flies, crane flies, native bees, spiders, assassin bugs, praying mantis, native flies to name a few. They all help keep my insect pests at bay in my organic vegetables. For this organic farmer they are my unforeseen heroes against insect pests. They're the easiest of all my friends. They don't talk back, I don't have to put on barbeques, or buy them beer, they don't tear up my house, I don't have to clean up after them, I don't have to feed them, take them for a walk, pet them, or bring them in at night, and there's no expensive veterinarian bills. All I have to do is provide them with flowers and habitat. At Sierra Valley Farms we have not sprayed pesticides of any kind on our certified organic "fields of twenty seven shades of greens" for over twenty years. My program here on the farm is to "companion plant" my crops (so they are compatible to each other) together, keep the weeds manageable, and after harvest, allow the greens to go to flower to attract my friends, these beneficial insects, and then allow the vegetables to go to seed (which I collect) and then mulch them back to the soil as my compost, which is my nutrient base for the next year. The sunflowers and wildflowers that I plant around the perimeter of the fields along with the natural rangeland is a wonderful host to the "good guy bugs." It's amazing to watch these guys in action, behind the scenes eating aphids, and thrips and other "bad guy bugs." They seem to just show up when they're needed and then disappear when they're not. These friends are my insurance policy, I' have to thank my lucky stars to have these shamrock super heroes that protect my twenty seven shades of green here on the farm.

Aqua Green

Time off the Farm

"Colorless green ideas sleep furiously"

Noam Chomsky

Like the old saying "All work and no play make Johnny a dull boy." isn't that the truth!" So if most farmers work way too much and never take time off, no wonder we can be dull. There's enough to be bummed about when US News rates farming and farm laborers as #8 on the list as one of the lowest paying jobs and Sam Greenspan a freelance columnist rated temporary farm workers as #6 least popular job in America. That will make any farmer dull and depressed. So you farmers take some time off and go have some fun!!!

Aqua green has a metaphysical meaning of letting yourself take a break, allow healing through play and being childlike and even silly. Aqua green is the selected color of the green spectrum for "Taking time off the Farm", to give you a break from the long busy season(s) of farm life, to go off and have some playtime and play like a child. Most farmers put in a 40 hour work week by Thursday and work 60-80 hour weeks trying to support their families making only pennies on the dollar for their hourly wage. It's a lifestyle, not a job, "you do what you have to do" to make ends meet and save the farm, the family and the farmer. It's what your forefathers before have done many generations before you, but in today's society Farmers have the highest suicide rates of any occupation and there's many reasons why. So farmers out there you had better take a break and take care of "Number One... you!"

Aqua green is the color we need to balance work and play. I know I put in 40 hours in the first three days of the work week, from April through October seven days a week. I attend at least four farmers markets a week, and harvesting, planting, weeding, and irrigating crops the rest of the week, up at 5 am, working all day and coming in from the fields at 9:30 pm. Then add to that: three barn dinners, running a full Friday Farmers market and coordinating three blues concerts here on the farm during that period. By November I'm ready for a break!

Growing up on the flower farm, mom and dad weren't much for taking long vacations. I can't remember them taking a couple of weeks off to travel or go anywhere. We did take a long four day weekend for Thanksgiving to come up to this farm to visit Grandma and the uncles, but it was mixed with work because we would go out on the ranch and cut bows of ponderosa pine limbs with the pine cones attached, to bring home for the flower market. It was fun when we were here, but the six to seven hour drive all four of us (Dad, Mom, Larry and Gary) packed in a 1948 one-ton GMC flat-bed truck wasn't very fun. The only fun we had on the drive was stopping at Denny's in Roseville to get a big chocolate milkshake.

I think where Mom and Dad got their pleasures and time off break was through weekly and monthly social events. They were very social, loved people and going to parties, dances and Italian social events after work and when we weren't spending the week ends on the farm. That was there aqua green, matter of fact turquoise was Mom's favorite gemstone, and Dad always wore this teal-aqua sports coat to all the events. It all makes sense now.

I believe it is very important for farmers to take time away from the farm with family or friends, or both. Sometimes it's hard to do because for me the farm becomes you, and I become the farm. I care more about the farm than me most times and that's dangerous for the soul. There were tough times for me financially and emotionally, time of depression when you feel like there's nowhere to turn, you find yourself digging deeper into a rut that you can't get out of because it's all around you on the farm and you can't get away from it. The farm is always staring you in the face, the good times and bad. It's good for a farmer and the mind to get off the farm, and just forget about the farm for a while. Whatever you do don't bring work and thoughts of the farm with you on vacation!

When you try and write books about farming and the farmers' lifestyle, most times it's positive, uplifting and inspirational. In todays' world farmers are so few and far between that from the outside looking in it looks glamourous, but there is a dark side that no one wants to hear about, or talk about that needs to be told and It's about farmer suicides.

The Guardian (December 6, 2017), wrote an article: Why are farmers killing themselves in record numbers? This was a shocking article for me to read but the statistics show that the suicide rate for farmers are more than double that of veterans. The CDC (Center for Disease Control) 2016 study also supported these suicide statistics and found people working in agriculture (farms, laborers, ranchers, fisherman, and logging) take their lives at a rate five times higher than any other occupation. You never hear about this in the news because farmers today make up less than one percent of all American occupations, but these numbers are staggering. The overwhelming problem is caused by stress, the feeling of no way out, failure and disappointment. Dr Rosmann an Iowa farmer, is a psychologist and has been studying why farmers are taking their lives for over 40 years at such alarming rates and currently higher than any other occupation. Rosmann has concluded that the stresses from the farm are: financial, overworked, under-appreciated, unhappily married, in debt, can't afford insurance, no benefits and no incentives. He also stated that the rates could be even higher than that because many deaths are considered agricultural accidents to disguise their suicides. We are not alone, an Australian farmer dies by suicide every four days, and in the UK, one farmer takes his/her life every week, and in France every two days, and in India more than 270,000 farmers have committed suicide since 1995.

Why? Rosmann states that the number one cause is loss of the family farm. In the modern era, in the 1980's, the market prices crashed, loans were called it and interest rates doubled overnight. Farmers were forced to liquidate their operations and evicted from their land. That's when suicide rates began to soar. In the spring of 1985, farmers descended on Washington D. C. by the thousands. For weeks they stayed in tents on the Mall, surrounding the White House and marched along Pennsylvania Avenue with signs, each with the name of a farmer or rancher that had committed suicide or lost their land, these signs were then staked into the lawn around the White House. It was said that there were so many of these signs that it looked like a cemetery.

Rosmann said that "Farmers just did not deal with revealing their tender feelings." "They felt like failures", Rosmann said, and it continues today. Rosmann then began a free hotline for Midwest farmers to get counseling and started a nationwide program called Farm and Ranch Stress Assistance Network (FRSAN) as part of the 2008 Farm Bill, but it never got funded. Rosmann said that the Republicans claimed it was an unnecessary expenditure which would increase the national debt, while also saying "healthy farmers are the most important asset to agricultural production (sound familiar?)." Thank you GOP! Again you fail the small American Farmer! As of 2014 there is no federal funding for any suicide support group for farmers, and farmers are still the leading occupation for suicides. Well fellow farmers don't be a statistic! Get help if you need it, and take time off the farm to take care of Number one—You!

It took me a while when I was young to take time off for Number one—Me. The concept of not thinking about the farm while I was on vacation was hard to do, because around mom and dad it was always about the flower farm and work, work, work, but once I did about 30 years ago, it was easy to, "allow healing through play and being child-like and even silly., and with the friends I have that was scary." It was beyond silly! I'm the total opposite of Mom and Dad when it comes to enjoying time off the farm. I'm not much for small talk at social events even though I am very social, it's that I spend all spring, summer and early fall talking to a lot of people at all the farmers markets that I attend, and being the "host with the most" at our "farm-to fork "barn dinners and dancing away at our blues concerts, so for me I just want to get away from the small talk and spend time with my special friends, forget the farm and be childlike and silly!

You know the beer commercial about the Dos Equis guy..."the most interesting man in the world...drink thirsty my friend." Well I twist that a little bit to explain my friends. Instead I call my friends ..."the most interesting friends in the world...and we drink "thirsty my friend!" You know over the years there's that special friend you grew up with that was your best friend in high school or your childhood best friend that you may not see them for a while, but when you do it's like you never left, "you continue where you left off." Well I don't have only one or two I have seven and a few that have come around after these seven. It's not my "seven shades of friends", but instead I have "seven shady friends!" They are all so unique in very different ways and we get together for different vacations, other than that we have our separate lives and save up for getting together for special trips. It's my time to get off the farm and un-wind-- My salvation.

My seven friends are (first name or nickname to protect the guilty!) "Uncle Bob", Terry, "Chic", Mark," Fish Bait", "Skate-"Eddie Bauer Boy", and Bob. The amazing thing is that only Bob and "Uncle Bob" are still married and the most normal of the bunch, then you throw the rest of us in with the bathwater as being, single (never married), or divorced and still single today in the over 60 club. We all met in college except "Fish Bait", who was in my Junior High class in Redwood City, and have stayed friends ever since. I was never one to join clubs (like Rotary, Elks etc.), because one: I never had time, and two: I didn't like all the "bullshit antics you play" at the meetings. So all of us friends just got together to party, laugh and "do something outdoors."

The Fish Trip

The infamous annual fish trip hiking down the Middle Fork of the Feather River was the most popular fishing trip since the late 1970's. As we got older, in the last ten years we old guys tend to car camp to other mountain lakes as our legs can't keep up with the rigorous hikes anymore. If there was ever a trip that represents Aqua green to "allow healing through play and being childlike and even silly", this was the trip!

This was a typical Feather River trip in 1986. Fish bait, Chic, Skate (Eddie Bauer boy), and myself. We were all going to meet at the trailhead above La Porte, Ca. park our vehicles at our secret spot and hike down to the middle fork of the Feather River. "Chic" was my old roommate at Cal Poly, San Luis Obispo, he got his nickname from chicollini (Chico) from the Marks Brothers, because he looked like him. "Chic" was an engineer, short-stocky, very sure of himself, Sicilian, loves women, and to hunt and go fishing, pretty much in that order. We would be puzzled about Chic's decision making process, because it wasn't the norm; as I describe him as "he was just short of genius, but a mile from common sense." We would just shake our heads and laugh, when he would try to rationalize something totally "off-the-wall" and all we could say was "that's just chic" he's never going to change. Then came "Fish bait" (FB), I named him that because I would tease him about the fish he would catch were so small. About the size you would use for fish bait, like minnows. FB worked in the computer industry in sales, and "knew it all." We would say…"If you want to know about anything just ask FB he knows it all", then you would have a twenty minute argument about something he knew nothing about. Last was Skate (Eddie Bauer boy), we all named him Skate because in his early years he had a job as a skating waiter at a French restaurant in Palo Alto, and the Eddie Bauer boy title came from Skate always having the latest gadgets for camping, hiking, or fishing. He was a tall "Swede", fireman, strong as an ox, a loner, Skate would wonder off on his own for hours, then at night have to sleep "anywhere" that was away from camp. It was just Skate. Well as for me they just called me Romano, I didn't really have a nickname, and I was just the instigator then the peacemaker of the bunch. There was always had a rival between all of us as who was going to be "King Fish", the one on the fishing trip that would catch the biggest fish.

On this trip, we started out by burying a small cooler full of Ice and about six beers about a foot in the ground at the start of the trail and covered it with distinguished rocks so that on our way out we could find it and have some "cold ones." We backpacked down a grueling five mile trail, straight down to the Feather River which took us about six hours. During normal years in early June it was an uneventful hike, but on this trip we encountered about four timber rattlers along the trail, which we shot with our pistol loaded with .22 snake shot. It's a very eerie feeling when you hear them rattle yards in front of you and you can't find where they are at that moment. Chic and Fish bait would always pack way to heavy so they spent most of the hike on their back, falling down most of the trip and Skate and I would have to take some of their "crap" to lighten their load. Skate and I always travelled light.

The river was high that year, with a lot of debris in the river, we always set camp on the other side of the river, so this year, we had to wade across, Skate the taller and strongest of the four, shuttled the packs to the other side and Chic, Fish bait and I stumbled across, falling in, and then just swimming across. We then set up camp, lit a bon fire, got drunk, and picked on each other all night long, and laughed until our stomach hurt over just "stupid" stuff. The next morning Chic made a great breakfast, as he always did, with eggs, bacon, coffee, and linguica and Fish bait and Skate spent the morning hours setting up their fly fishing gear, Chic and I would have a couple of "belts" of grappa, or whiskey in the morning and laugh at them for wasting their time on fishing gear because they weren't going to catch any fish anyway. By mid-morning we all were off fishing on-our own in every direction and were to meet back at camp for "happy-hour", which Chic would yell out at the top of his lungs every time you saw him, "Happy Hour!" Chic would never go without a beer or a cocktail in his hand the whole trip. Later that morning I came around a bend in the river and there was Fish bait as so often happened to him trying to untangle a "birds nest" (what a big tangle in your fishing line looks like) .and swearing to himself "Got damn it", and making excuses why it happened, as I passed him heading upstream. The boys would laugh at me because I don't fly fish and just use spinners and float natural bait, they were all very good fly fisherman, but I would catch just as many as them for less the effort. At the end of the day we all met for happy hour lying about the fish that got away. We all caught nice fish 17 to 21 inchers, and by midday Skate had the biggest fish so far. By sunset Chic and I were usually done with fishing and ready for a real "Happy hour", and getting camp ready for dinner. As we headed back to camp Chic shot a big timber rattler along the river, so

I said,

"Lets' play a trick on Fish bait, and cut the rattlesnakes head off and coil it on his pillow, he'll never see it until he lights his little candle, and will shit his pants(FB was very protective of all his gear, never sharing anything, but bumming all your stuff)!"

We called Fish Bait "camp slug", because he was notorious for would fishing till dark never contributing to camp (cooking, clean-up, get wood, start a fire etc.), the rattlesnake on his pillow would be his award for being "camp slug." So that night we all had dinner, drank, smoked a little ganja, and cooked our trout, (it was always entertaining watching Fish bait make trout almandine, spending hours on it, only to have it fall in the fire, charred, and full of charcoal and ash). Chic had slipped off pretending to get some fire wood only to go and coil the rattle snake on Fish baits' pillow. It was getting past midnight and we all made the excuses that it was time to go to bed, and as we retired to our sleeping bags, we could here Fish bait stumbling and scrounging around his camp to light his little candle, then silence for a few minutes and then we saw the glow and glimmer of the candle, waiting in total anticipation of the moment, well it came. Suddenly we here Fish bait shout,

"Holy-Shit…What the fuck!" Fish bait came running toward the bon fire hyperventilating…

"There's….There's…a…a…" then we all started laughing hysterically, and he realized the prank. "You Assholes…he said!

The next day we determined that Fish bait was "King Fish" for the trip as his trout out-measured Skate's by a nose. Fish bait and Chic had to get back to work, so Skate and I were going to stay a couple more days. After the boys left Skate and I decided to go look for firewood and we began to scour the county side for downed, dry wood and haul it back to camp. We found this old skid trail and followed it to see where it would go and about a hundred yards up; we could hear a rattle, and a sudden braking of branches and a ferocious growl brake into the open, charging full speed at us, it was a huge pit bull, Skate grabbed a log, I drew my .38 pistol and sighted in him at about twenty five yards and he was on a death march right at us, then to his defense, his owner pops out of the brush and yells

"Bull Dozer freeze…don't shoot!"

Luckily he froze and Skate lower the log and I withdrew my pistol and we looked at each other and said

"Fuck!"

The pit bull retreated to the owner, and we met up with him, he was apologetic and offered us some ganja back where he and his wife were collecting wood. We visited with them awhile then Skate and I headed back to camp. Enough excitement for the day!

We stayed a couple more days but the trout had quit biting, and we were running out of food, so we decided to pack up camp and leave the next morning. Skate knew of a short cut to get up to the road, then cut back to the trail head where our vehicles were, it was an old deer trail. It was straight up, we were young then and it was slow going but not a problem, we were almost to the top where there was a fork in the trail and we heard voices coming from the other direction on the trail, sounding closer and closer, then we yelled out

"Hey...who's there?"

"Hey what's up, be there in a second", they replied.

As they emerged from the brush, there were two guys in dress suits and leather shoes, dragging suit cases, with another gal dressed in slacks (you can't make this shit up I swear!), they were all dirty, covered in "stickers", with twigs stuck in their hair, their suits were torn and tattered, then

Skate said

"What the hell are you guys doing out here all dressed up?"

They said

"Well, we're from Boston and were in Chico for a wedding and some friends told us about this river so we packed in all this food about two miles upriver, but we couldn't eat it all so we left it there for the bears, with a sign on it... 'Food for the Bears!"

They had left pies, desserts, steaks, all kind of food, and Skate and I looked at each other and said,

"Hell, here we are eating Top Romen and shitty dried sodium food, when if we would have fished a little more upstream we would have had a feast fit for kings...Wow!"

They followed us up to the road then hitched a ride back to Chico, and Skate and I found our vehicles, the dug up our small cooler of ice "cold beers", hung out for a while reminiscing the events of the "Fish Trip", then said our good bye, "Until Next year" I said. You just can't make this shit up. I was ready to go back to the farm.

All farmers, men and women need a release from the farm, whether it's a group of women friends going on a nature hike in the woods for a week or a shopping spree in the big city, or taking the family on a vacation or even attending farming conferences and workshops during the slow season to keep up the motivation and spark new life into the farm when you get back. The farm's always going to be waiting for you when you get back so enjoy yourself while you are gone.

Spring Training

Well you can guess what this is all about, the boys going to drink beer, acting silly and watching baseball. The busy lifestyle of a farmer is always 24/7, and especially during major league baseball season. I love my San Francisco Giants but I never get to go see them at their beautiful field at Oracle Park in San Francisco because its farm season. So about twenty five years ago some friends had season tickets to spring training in Scottsdale Arizona during the month of March and invited me to go. I was hooked on spring training after that! My other "non-fish trip" buddies, Terry (my partner in crime), and Bob (Truckee), would pile into a Motel 6 ("seis"…as we pronounced it!), along with a few drop ins like Gordon, Rob, Angelo, and Mark, (for a couple days) and we would stay for seven to ten days religiously every year going to baseball games, making total fouls of our selves partying and hanging out with the beer vendors, and just having fun not worrying about our daily lives at home or on the farm.

Over the years we've become very good friends with all of the beer vendors (I wonder why?), especially "Beer-man Dave" as we called him, otherwise known as Molokai Dave. After the games we would join up with Dave and five or six other beer vendors and hang out at our favorite pubs, drink beer, watch the "Final Four" in basketball on TV, and discuss baseball, our "real jobs" and life. We had become regulars. The beer vendors were a lot like farmers', they loved what they did, and didn't make much money doing it, but looked forward to doing their job every spring. I could definitely relate, they're dedication as vendors were as strong as mine as a farmer

As I got older partying was not the only reason to go to spring training but also to collect baseballs. My son Joey was in little league, then travel ball, and high school baseball. He's a left handed pitcher still today (recruited by California Lutheran University to play baseball 2016) playing baseball in southern California. We live in a very rural part of northeastern California and Joey played in Portola, California. In these rural towns, there's no money to support youth programs and it all falls on the parents, bake sales, and "hand-me-downs." That goes for uniforms and buying baseballs. So over the last five years, I'm getting too old to sleep on the floor of a Motel 6 ("seis"), so we've "all pitched in" to rent a condo for a month and we all share it different times of the spring training season during the month of March. Terry and I stay the longest usually about three weeks, and we love to play practical jokes on ourselves and "play fun on others", laugh and most of all visit the practice facilities of all the baseball clubs that are within thirty miles of Scottsdale. We're early risers, so we go early and "shag baseballs." We collect as many as we can each year now and I donate them to all the little league coaches in my area. It's funny to watch two old fat guys chasing baseballs across the parking lots of these ball parks. If there are little kids around we let them have them, usually they out run us anyway. We still party with the beer vendors, but a lot of them can't "run the stairs" anymore with buckets of beer anymore. Then it's time to "hit the pavement running", the party's over! It is time to Farm.

Maui

The fish trip and spring training were for me and the boys, no wives or girlfriends allowed. But when you're a farmer you have to make time for family. Maui was our get-a-way family time. Kim's folks had a place in Maui in July. The heart of farming season and I couldn't go most times, but I always felt that it was important that Kim and Joey (even as a baby) get off the farm and enjoy themselves in Maui for a couple of weeks and they did, because farming was my dream and I knew it wasn't hers. As years passed Kim and I bought a timeshare of our own in October for our family to go to Maui during our slower farm time of the year. Today even though Kim and I aren't together anymore, we split the condo, each staying there every other year. I still go by myself most times for a week or two, but unlike my other two fun trips this one is to focus on the farm, away from the farm, reflect and assess the year we've had at Sierra Valley Farms and write books like these. Maui is my balance of work and play, not playing so hard anymore but transitioning into the golden years ahead of me.

Having fun on the farm! All the kids.

Jade Green

The Golden Years

"Our wisdom is stored in the Trees"

Santosh Kalwar

Ah...the Golden years, a time of reflection for me. Jade green indicates a generosity of spirit, giving without expecting anything in return. Jade green increases worldly wisdom and understanding, assisting in the search of enlightenment, friendship, sincerity, sympathy, harmony, good health, and hope. Jade is the color of immortality, a time to reflect on life, and decreases fatigue, depression and anxiety.

Small farmers today are farming well into their golden years. The average age of the farmer is 62 years of age and many are farming well into their late seventies. The lack of new farmers taking over farmers is putting pressure on the older farmers to continue to farm. For many of these older farmers the farm and social security is all they have for retirement, it's all they've ever done...they are the farm.

I remember when Grandpa Romano (we would call him Nonno, means Grandpa in Italian) would sit in his old rocking chair, with his felt Fedora (Mafia style) hat on, talking in Italian to his "paisano's", his Toscana cigar fumigating the patio, drinking grappa, and ranting and raving about the Roosevelt years, and how Rocky Marciano was the greatest fighter ever. My brother Larry and I would sit there for hours in awe and "green envy" of their wisdom, knowledge and love of life.

Nonno Romano was our mentor; he stood for everything we believed we knew at seven years old. When we got home from the flower farm, Larry and I would run right over to Nonno's and he would have a wonderful dinner waiting for us plus some great gelato. Nonno was a great cook, he had to be, because Grandma died in 1933 of a mastoid infection in her ear and Nonno raised dad and his two sisters (Inez and Mary) by himself in that little 800 square foot house he built in 1921 in Redwood City, California. We would sit on the couch with Nonno and he would tell us stories in part-Italian-part-English, about the "old country" (Italy) and what is was like coming to America as an immigrant. He was pretty smart, he would give Larry and I a juice glass of half wine and half water and after listening to his stories, and finishing that juice glass of water and wine, we were "out like a light", Nonno would then call Dad next door and say "Luigi ...coma getta u boys.." and him or Mom would come and take us home, it was bed time. Mind you we were about eight or nine years old at the time. He wasn't the happiest grandfather to my cousins, but we were his favorites, I think because we worked hard on the farm with Mom and Dad in the flower business that he started in 1921, and that Mom and Dad took it over when he retired in 1964.

Nonno Romano cherished his Golden years; by 1964 he was done farming full-time (at least on paper) and turned the reins over to Dad to continue G. L. Romano & Son Wholesale Florist at the San Francisco Flower Market and at the flower farm in San Jose. In a traditional Old Italian family like ours, it's a lot like the movie Godfather, the grandfather is always "head-honcho", respected until the day they die. What Nonno says, "Goes", no argument, even though he turned over the reins to Dad he still influenced the business and family whether Mom and Dad liked it or not. There was some friction and a few Italian swears words exchanged between Nonno and Dad on occasion at the farm.

The color jade green best represents the Golden years, especially for Dad and I, not necessarily for Nonno Romano. Jade gives you the wisdom to be able and see past self-imposed limitations and bring prosperity and abundance into your life Mom and Dad are definitely all of the above; they were saints, when it comes to dealing with Nonno Romano!

Nonno Romano had his good points, but driving wasn't one of them, especially during his Golden years. He was a terrible driver, and as he got up in age he started to get arthritis in the joints of his hands and feet and that didn't help his driving any. He would pick us up from the farm in San Jose on Sundays in his Jade-Blue (yes…it was jade blue!) 1962 two-door Chevy Impala, bombing down this dirt road, dust flying and horn blowing…Larry and I knew that it was time to go home! We loved to see Nonno on Sundays because that meant we could leave the farm at about 3 pm instead of coming home with Mom and Dad at 6pm. It was a treacherous drive though; Nonno would swear at the other drivers, shake his fist at them and swear in Italian "fung culo", which means "Up your ass!" It didn't help matters on the freeway for sure, and Larry and I would slide down below the seat in embarrassment.

It was late October, pumpkin season. Dad would give Larry and me an acre of ground to grow tomatoes, pumpkins and gourds to sell at the flower market as our "school money" for college and buying our own work clothes, boots and few nice things for ourselves. On this day we went to the farm in two trucks, Dad took the old 1948 GMC one-ton to load the flowers and Nonno took the 1965 GMC half-ton that had these high plywood sides so that we could load as many pumpkins as possible. At the end of the day were we loaded to the "gills" with pumpkins, and Larry and I hopped in the truck with Nonno and off we went with this overload of pumpkins. The 65' pick up was the old "three-on-the-tree" stick shift on the steering column, It was a new advancement for trucks in that era and Nonno first didn't like it and second couldn't get it in the right gear, only to add more problems on the highway with people flipping us off and blowing the horn profusely because we were going to slow. I had driven the truck many times on the farm and I liked driving, Larry wasn't much for driving or operating equipment on the farm. So about five miles of this chaos, and mayhem, Nonno pulls over and He said to me:

"Hey Gary you drive."

"Nonno, I can't drive, I'm only fourteen." I said,

"Ah you drive on the ranch. Drive!"

So I slid over to the drivers' seat, barely tall enough to reach the clutch and peak over the steering wheel, and took off as fast as I could to merge on Highway 101, "Blood Alley" as it was called then (for a reason!) because the speed limit was 70 miles an hour. About twenty minutes into the drive home, who passes me but Mom and Dad. You should have seen the look on Mom's face! I'm sure she said a few Hail Mary's on the way home! I had never driven seventy miles an hour before, and now I had to maneuver the Marsh Road off-ramp in Menlo Park. I downshifted, but was still going a little too fast. As I took the curve I could feel the overload of pumpkins shift on the truck and as we turned the truck leaned way over and we swayed around the curve, trying not to over-correct, I kept the truck under control and navigated the exit. The last thing I wanted to do was roll the truck full of pumpkins on the off ramp, and that would not be good. We made it home in one piece, and I didn't get busted by the cops, and that's all I cared about. Larry and Nonno were laughing at me through this whole ordeal and when I parked the truck in the driveway as Mom and Dad stood at the gate with a sigh of relief that I made it home in one piece. As I was getting out of the truck Nonno leaned over and said "Our secret…I say nothing about Marsh Road…you did good!" That was Nonno he did whatever he wanted and didn't care if it was right or wrong.

Nonno's Golden years were spent mostly at home, his health wasn't good, so he ended up moving into my room during my high school years, I slept on a day bed in the dining room (that we hardly used) for about three years. It was hard on Mom especially because after working all day on the farm she would have to cook for him and clean up after him, and Nonno was grumpy and didn't treat her very nice. He later got a stroke at 82 and we moved him back to his little house and hired a full-time Samoan woman "Jane" to take care of him but he died at 84 in his home in 1975. I realized at an early age and especially coming from a strong Italian family, that the grand parents are first priority. Mom and Dad and Larry and I spent a lot of time with Nonno during the last few years of his life and he was the happiest just spending time with family, grand kids, and being comfortable in his own home, not in some convalescent home where nobody comes to see you and your just room 265B.

We were the typical farming family in those days 1950's well into the 1970's. All the small farmers had the family unit present on their farms. The evenings were spent sitting down for dinner that mom, auntie and grandma cooked for the "boys" when they came in off the farm or the ranch. After dinner the kids played outside and the adults sat around on the porch and had cocktails and engaged in long conversations about the farm, politics and the economy, or whatever else gossip was going on in the community. Those were different times than today.

I remember Mom, Dad, Larry and I were at Purity Market in Menlo Park shopping for groceries on our way to the flower farm on this Saturday morning in July 1975. Nonno had just passed away about a month before and Dad had always been a smoker then, smoking Tareyton cigarettes and a Tiparillo cigar once in a while. Over the years on the farm when Nonno was there Dad would get frustrated with Nonno, and get mad and pass it on to us kids, especially when we were helping him. He would have a short fuse and if Dad asked you to go retrieve something in the shop like a pipe wrench or a pipe fitting, you had better know what it is, where it is, and you RAN, not walked to get it. On this day in the grocery store Mom was by his side and Dad picked up a carton of

Tareyton as he always did and placed it in the shopping cart and walked about three steps past the cigarette section then he stopped, retrieved the carton of cigarettes from the shopping cart and put it back on the shelf and Dad has not touched a cigarette since that moment in 1975 when he was 50. Since that day not only did he quit smoking, but he never raised his voice at us kids ever again, and became the most positive, uplifting person I know, always smiling, loves the ladies, laughing with a grin "ear-to-ear." still today in 2019 at 92.

The pressure of "Nonno running the show" was off Dad and Mom, especially Dad, being the only son, now he didn't have the "ball and chain" to drag around, he could be the person he always wanted to be. Mom and Dad continued full speed ahead at the farm through the "Hay days" of the 1980's and well into the 1990's and by 1995 the flower market had changed and all the flower shippers were out of business because of the laws of NAFTA opening up the markets for cheap South American flowers had inundated the flower market. Mom and Dad struggled to keep the farm in Morgan Hill and decided to sell the farm in 1995. Mom was 71 and Dad was 69. They wanted to slow down and keep working but not so hard. They sold the farm and made an arrangement with the new owners (Chinese vegetable growers), that they would be able to go back and cut the blossoms of the pussy willow, flowering quince, and peach blossoms for the next ten years for a set price. I had moved to Lake Tahoe and was working for Parks and Recreation while Larry helped Mom and Dad at the flower market until Larry died in 1997 of AIDS, and that hit the family hard, he was only 39 years old. At the time Mom was 73 and Dad was 71 and I would take time to come down on my days off to help.

Mom and Dad really enjoyed their Golden years together. After they sold the farm, Dad kept the stall: G. L. Romano & Son Wholesale Florist at the flower market to sell what he cut off the old farm and what Mom and Dad would find along the roadsides. They always wanted to keep working; the word retirement was not in the Romano's vocabulary or dictionary then or today. They loved to hop in the truck and take a ride to the mountains, and cut berries, collect old bird nests, or downed oak and pine limbs that had lichen and moss on them to sell at the flower market. During their evening they enjoyed going to the Italian Catholic Federation (ICF) and Sons of Italy dinners, and dances with their neighbors the Marcucci's. They had a great balance of work and play until 2010 when mom fell and broke her hip and dementia kicked in really fast and Dad took care of her until she passed away at 89 in 2014. What I observed from them during the last twenty golden years of their lives together was to enjoy life and "don't sweat-the-small-stuff"; they enjoyed life and people of all colors and creed and never made judgment on anyone. Now that Mom and Larry are both gone our immediate family has dwindled down to just me and Dad, here on the farm and Tami (my first ex-wife) and our daughter Elizabeth live in Florida and Kim (my second ex-wife) and our son Joey live in southern California Like most families today my farming family is just Dad and I here on the farm and Chloe my lab, and I am divorced and. I really didn't know how Dad would react to Mom's death because Mom never drove and they did everything together, work and play. It was tough for Dad the first week, he's an emotional guy anyway and the funeral services were hard for him to handle, and also for the rest of us. I really didn't know what to expect, because he was born in Nonnos' old house next store by a midwife and when Mom and Dad got married they built the house I was raised in next store. He had never lived anywhere else, and the sentimental value seemed overwhelming, and we had been renting Nonnos' little old house since he died in 1975. A few days after the service,

I said

"Dad, what do you want to do? Stay in Redwood City or move to the farm?"

He paused a second and looked surprised that I would invite him to the farm and Dad replied

"Hell, I want to move to the farm, of course!"

Dad then continued to say,

"You know I've out lived all my neighbors, and most of my friends, and the neighborhood is all changed I don't really know anybody anymore."

"I want to go up there with you and Joey (when Joey comes home for the holidays and summers from college)."

I said,

"Great...sure come on up I have the Guest Cottage that you can move into."

Dad said

"Well then, I have a lot of work to do to sell these two places...I had better get busy."

Dad was ready to spend the rest of his days here on the farm, and be an active participant at Sierra Valley Farms. Dad, or better known as "Lou" as most people call him, didn't waste any time getting things organized for a grandiose exit from Redwood City, Dad wanted to sell everything fast and "exit stage left" as soon as possible, "time was a wasting!" Over the next three weeks he coordinated some antique ladies from Roseville, California to buy most of the expensive furniture and antiques that Mom had, and these Pilipino women from the East Bay by Oakland came and bought pretty much everything else. I came down to do a weekend yard sale with Dad a couple months later and there wasn't much left. He even sold his little Ford Ranger pickup; I guess he figured that he would just ride back with me when the houses were listed on the market. The 89 year old Lou Romano was on a mission to relocate to Beckwourth, California.

It took a couple months to give notice to the tenants in Nonnos' old house for them to relocate and for the realtor to get the houses listed on the market to sell. During those couple of months I got the guest house ready for my new tenant, Lou Romano. It was across the driveway from my house a one-bedroom studio, about 750 square feet, with French doors that looked over Sierra Valley. The morning sunrise would wake you up at 5 am coming right through those French doors and I knew Dad would love having his cup of coffee and watching our spectacular morning sunrises.

Mom passed away in February of 2014, and on May 1, I drove my high box produce truck down and we rented a twenty-one foot U-Haul, and some buddies help load it and Lou and I were off the next morning to his new home at Sierra Valley Farms. Dad had taken care of Mom for about four years full time, she was pretty much out of it, and had to do all the cooking, help her to bed, and help with her hygiene, on top of that she had dementia pretty bad and couldn't keep a conversation. Despite it all Dad was not going to put her in a nursing home. When she was in the rehabilitation hospital for three months after she fell and broke her hip Dad was with her day and night and would just go home to sleep and be back the next morning. Dad definitely paid his dues and I think wanted to turn over a new chapter in his life and be Lou Romano.

For me I wanted to make sure Dad would enjoy the last of his Golden years here on the Farm. I knew he wanted "to farm again." Lou wanted to get on that tractor at 89 and disk away, and he was in great shape, only had been in the hospital once in his life. The burden of taking care of Mom was off his shoulder, she was in a better place now being taken care of, and Dad was going to enjoy life. Mom was always like a "governor" on a throttle that just "let dad go so fast", keeping him in range, but now the governor was off and the throttle was full speed ahead, here comes Lou Romano!

The timing was perfect, Joey was off to college and it was just Dad and I and Chloe (my Labrador) on the farm. We got back to the farm and spent the week getting Dad in his new home and put the rest in storage. Dad and I are very similar in personality, very outgoing, we get along, never argue, and very friendly, but there was a side of Dad that I didn't really know and that was he was not only a "chick-magnet", better than having a golden retriever puppy, the women love him, of all ages (He's a very attractive man at his age), but he has that charm that only a few people have, my brother Larry had it, you're born with it, people are just attracted to you and Dad's got it. Whenever we would go anywhere people would come out of the wood work to talk to him, he was like a magnet.

During the first few months with Dad on the farm and me pushing 60 it made me reflect how I was going to spend my Golden years, and I thought it was pretty special that we both are spending our Golden years together. What better way to spend it farming together, with "the legend" from the flower market, my Dad, Lou Romano. After being around Dad so much over the first few months I asked,

"How do you stay so happy, always smiling?"

Dad replied

"I just like people, I like to work, and don't worry about anything, it all works out."

Simple as that! Dad has found the secret to living a long productive life and the key is to be happy, stay active in what you love and do everything in moderation. As I enter my Golden years I'm starting to slow down and just grow the crops that I enjoy growing (most of my 27 shades of green), sell only to the chef's and restaurants I enjoy working with, and go to only the farmers markets that I enjoy going to. Since Dad has been here on the farm I'm really enjoying life, enjoying watching and learning from Dad, his wisdom and how to live life to your fullest and I like being there for him to make his life as comfortable as possible.

I truly believe that the young farmers today really need to spend their time around the 'old-time farmers, to picked their brains on the old ways and absorb their wisdom because once it's gone that knowledge and experience can't be replaced by technology or formal education. There's the human element of the aged farmer that's the intangible here. There's the life of the farmer, the story that he tells to the young farmer is what that young farmers is going to remember the most, the impression that the aged farmer leaves on the new inspiring farmer is priceless.

There's a new dynamic that is happening here on the farm and that's a "role-reversal" if you will, when I was growing up on the farm with mom and dad they really pushed my brother Larry and I very hard while we were working in the fields…well now it's my turn to give dad the orders on the daily work schedule here at Sierra Valley Farms. Do I feel that it's time for a little payback for all the times dad yelled at me to work harder, or deprived me of playing little league because I had to help on the flower farm? I only thought about it for a split second… of course not. I would never want to put a heavy work load on my 90 year old dad!! It is funny though how now the roles are reversed that I am giving him the "to do list" in the morning over coffee instead of him telling me what to do. It took me a while to feel comfortable doing that.

After only two years here were like "two peas in a pod" and has become the farm's biggest celebrity. Lou is an Icon to the locals around the Reno/Lake Tahoe area. He has his own FB page "Uncle Louie"; he's got a local IPA beer named after him at our local brewery so you can go and have a "Louie" after work; he's the main man at our weekly Farmers market here on the farm, as we advertise to "Go have a glass of wine with Uncle Louie!" He is also the main attraction at our farm-to-fork barn dinners, everyone wants to kiss Lou and get their "selfies" with him, also to meet and talk to Lou about his wisdom of farming for 90 plus years. Lastly, the women have to take a number at our blues concerts, in order to get a dance with Uncle Louie, there are always three or four dancing with him while he's grinning "ear-to-ear" Lou's definitely got it going! I'm pretty much "chump-change" when Lou's around and I hate to go out to dinner with Dad because they think were brothers, gee…"He looks 61, I look 92"…hmmm, I don't like that scenario, but Lou loves it! Who would have thought that my Dad would be the best marketing tool ever, and if I have to look 92 at 61, so be it, I can live with that, just think how good I'll look at 90!

I think Lou is a great example for all parents taking care of an elderly family member, that it is very important for seniors to have a purpose in life. They need to wake up every morning knowing they are valuable and can be productive, and go to bed at night feeling good about themselves and look forward to waking up the next morning and having a "to do list" that they can be excited about performing a job or even a simple task and hear a family member say…"thanks Dad for watering the garden or picking tomatoes," whatever their task may be. I think every senior living facility should have a small community garden within their courtyard, or even some simple planter bed or containers that the seniors can "putt-around in" planting flowers or vegetables, weeding and watering, taking care of the beds and then harvesting some greens or vegetables that can be given to the kitchen to be put in their dinners. You would be amazed how much pleasure it would bring to those seniors, but I've yet to see one in any senior living facility. You have to remember that these seniors that are 75 and older were raised during or just after the depression and World War II, and they remember the victory gardens that were put in in every community to grow food for their local towns and cities, so I think it would be very beneficial not only for the seniors that are able to take care, or participate in the gardens themselves, but even for those who cannot participate but can be wheeled into the gardens to observe the flowers, vegetables and the butterflies and that they are able to reminisce about those victory gardens of the past.

Looking back to generations at Nonno, and now Dad and how they chose to spend their Golden years is really dictated by the sign of the times. Nonno went to Chile first from Italy when he was fifteen years old, then to Ellis Island and then a boat ride to San Francisco to meet up with his brother and try and make a life in an unknown land, not knowing the language. The Italian immigrants were treated like dirt just like the, Irish, Germans, Polish and the Jews. Nonno would tell us how they called them WOP's (Without Papers) and Dago, Guinea and half the time they never got paid or were cheated on their wages. It was a hard life, and especially for Nonno, losing his wife at 33 and raising Dad and his two sisters through the depression and seeing all the changes of technology after WWII and into the 1970's. Nonno's Golden years were spent enjoying his immediate family especially us grand kids and a few neighbors that he liked and visiting the farm, that was all Giovanni Lodovico Romano wanted in his Golden years.

Mom and Dad's era was a little different, a little more upbeat, especially when you were as good looking as Dad was, he could have been a movie star, why the girls at Sequoia High School made him letter jacket that said, "The Lover" on the back, and no one knows what happened to the jacket we could never find it, but I bet Rose (my Mom) knows what happened to it, I'm sure she made short work of that jacket right into the hot burning stove! Out of high school dad went into the Navy right after WWII and then had to return to the marines a few years later in Korea after being a few days short of service for the Navy. I have a feeling Dad was a lot like his mother because Aunt Inez would say that Dad was a lot like her, easy going and happy. He then met Mom up here on the ranch in the late 1940's while Dad and Nonno were cutting pine bows and they were married in 1956 and had us twins in 1957. As mom and Dad raised us into the 1960's- 1990's those were "cool" times for raising kids, you came out of the Frank Sinatra era into Elvis and the Everly Brothers, and be "hip" with the hippies, hip hop, disco, rhythm and blues, and rock & roll. The times were changing not only in music but in technology. The "dot comers" came along, creating the computers age in Silicon Valley. Computers not only changed our world but how Americans were going to go about their everyday lives. During the beginning of Mom and Dads' Golden years in their late 60's they got out more than Nonno ever did and it wasn't only about work, they did more socialization, did go on a cruise, and were enjoying themselves with others, not like Nonno just staying home enjoying the grand kids. Mom and Dad definitely enjoyed their Golden years together and that chapter is closed and now Dad has a new chapter to add to his Golden years here on the farm.

Dad and I have our routine for the day, Lou gets up around 6:30 in the morning, and has his coffee and breakfast together, no I mean "together", he doesn't like milk, but likes cereal, so why not combine them, so he pours his coffee in his cereal," two birds with one-stone", it's an Italian thing! Lou then walks over to my place about 7:30 am and has another cup with me, visits with Chloe and we talk about the plan for the day on the farm, and Lou always starts the conversation with "What do you want me to do today?" Dad does most of my disking, and mowing. He bought himself a newer Kubota Utility tractor and a ride on mower so usually I get him fueled up and he's off mowing with his open road wide brimmed hat in his work clothes right after the morning dew has dried the fields. He works until it starts getting hot around 11:30 then he cleans up and heads into Portola (About 5 miles away and Lou just got his driver's license for another five years!) to have lunch with his buddies at the Veterans Hall for seniors ($2.50), then returns to the farm and if it's not too hot he will do some hula hoeing on the twenty seven shades of green, or continuing mowing or disking for me. If it's too hot he'll go inside and do word puzzles, or stick labels on my lettuce bags. Lou will say to me.

"I'm going to go and put on stickers"

I know what it means, he's always staying busy. Then in the late afternoon he'll watch the nature channel, Judge Judy, or Family Feud, depending what's on. About 4:30 he comes in for happy hour. Lou and I have our cocktail, usually brandy on the rocks, or if it's cold Lou will say

"I'll have a hot-toddy"

That' a shot of grappa, tablespoon of lemon juice, and honey in a cup, topped off with about three ounces of hot water. Then he'll sit on the couch and watch the local news, or the S.F. Giants, and always looking to see what the weather forecast will be for the week, and waiting for dinner, and I mean "waiting patiently for dinner." See, Mom spoiled Dad, she was the typical Italian wife, "waiting on her husband hands and feet", well when Mom broke her hip and had dementia Dad had to do everything, including the shopping and cooking and clean up, so I thought when Dad moved to the farm we would share the duties..."No-way", Lou likes to be waited on. It bothered me at first but as I thought about it, "Hey it's my privilege to wait on him and at 92, I'm just happy he's still got a sharp mind and functioning body, I mean he still does physical work, hops in the back of the truck and loads produce, or unloads empty boxes at the end of the day, plus dancing! On Wednesday nights during the summer, there is free music at a local restaurant in Graeagle, and about 6 pm Lou hops in the truck and goes and listens to music, joins his harem of woman for a glass of wine and conversation, then I see him pulling into his studio about 8:30 pm. Lou's amazing! Hell I'm the old mother hen around here I always say to him "Well be careful of deer, and come home before dark."

Lou was raised in the Redwood City, California known as having the best weather in the United States, there was a plaque on the City sign for years that said "Best by Government Test!", so when Dad spent the first winter here and I was worried that he might slip on the ice and snow and break a hip like Mom and then we would really be in trouble. How would I take care of him then? That following spring Joey got a full ride to play baseball at Cal Lutheran University in Thousand Oaks, in southern California. So when Joey had orientation to his new college I took Dad down there I thought to myself, "Maybe I should try to find a nice place (Assisted Living) for Dad to spend the winter, become a "snowbird." I didn't really know how to bring it up to him cordially, because I didn't want him to think that I was going to dump him in some "old folks home" where everyone's drooling and slumped over in a wheel chair and the place smells like urine. He also was so happy living on the farm and farming again. So awkwardly I asked Lou,

"What do think about Thousand Oaks?"

Lou replied,

"It's nice and warm here in the winter."

Lou had just opened the door for me and I said,

"Would you like to come down here for the winter, you could see Joey's baseball games, and just for a few months during the winter to get out of the snow then you come back to the farm when it's time to plant?"

Lou replied,

"Let's see if we can find a place."

So for the next few days we toured different Senior Assisted Living facilities and found the right one that Dad really liked. They call it a "short-stay" where you can stay for up to six months. So now I bring Dad down the end of October and pick him up in April, and after two years, of course, he now has a southern California harem to compliment his northern California harem.

On the drive back I told Lou,

"You know the good news about this place is that all the ladies have a little dementia, so when you come back, they'll think you never left." They'll say

"Lou we missed you yesterday"

And all you'll have to say is

"I went to see my son for a couple days."

He thought that was pretty funny and we laughed for a good while, then spent the rest of the drive talking about all the different farms we saw along the way back to the farm. Lou was now a snow bird.

Even at 92 Lou is still farming after all these years but he's had a little set back he was diagnosed with congestive heart failure, whereby your heart is "wearing out" basically and isn't as efficient pumping blood to your organs as it used to be, so he has to take it a little easier. Lou won't give up the tractor, no way! Before heading off to southern California last fall he met with his cardiologist, a very smart, nice young doctor and he explained to Lou that most likely he has a partial blockage in one of his arteries, and said the only way to find it and correct it is to do angio plasty and if they find the blockage they'll have to perform open heart surgery and at 91 (at the time) you may not come out of it at your age. The doctor said

"Lou, you'll have to decide what you want to do?"

Lou looked at me then turned to the young doctor and said

"Doc...what would you do if you were me?'

The doctor looked at Lou up and down, smiled and with a chuckle he said

"Lou if I looked like you; and can get around and be as productive as you are; with that attitude and smile...I wouldn't do a damn thing!"

On the ride home from Reno Dad wanted to make sure I knew that he wanted to go out of this world on a tractor or farming. Lou said

"Gary If I die on that tractor, that's the way I want to go!"

I laughed and said,

"I figured that, me too!"

As we turned in the driveway I said,

"You know dad...the good news is that these new tractors today automatically shut off if you fall off, so if I hear your Kubota tractor shut off I'll know you've joined Mom "on the big farm in the Sky!"

I finished by saying,

"If you were on the old Green Acres tractor (from the flower farm) it wouldn't stop and you might end up in Reno!"

That next morning in October I had pulled all the drip lines and took down all the deer fencing, it was time to mulch the fields of green, and disk them under for winter before taking Lou down to southern California. I got Lou set up with the mower on his Kubota tractor and off he went mulching the twenty seven shades of green, then after lunch I switched him onto the big John Deere with the disk and away he went grinning "ear-to-ear", disking away; the dust flying, his one hand on the back of the wheel well, the other on the steering wheel as he looks back at the rows of turned soil, followed by a cloud of dust and about fifty blackbirds as if he was throwing out bird seed. I know what Lou's feeling right now; it's the same way I feel when I disk. Lou has died and gone to heaven! I knew at that moment this is the way Lou would ride off into the sunset, as he drove past me to disk another field, he waved with his open road- wide brim hat, covered in dust with only his piercing bright green eyes wide open and his teeth half covered in Sierra Valley dirt that filled a smile like he had won the lottery. Lou is doing what he does best--Farm.

So that is my Golden years so far here on the farm, taking care of Chloe and Dad and making sure Lou is comfortable during the last of his Golden years. When Dad's gone (there's a good chance he could out live me!), my plan is to move in his studio and mentor a young couple to take over the farm. They can move in the main house and run the farm and I can "come and go" as I please spending the summers here and taking time off in the winter and off season to go to spring training, Maui, and travel a bit, and who knows, I might someday even meet the woman of my dreams!.

So now when somebody asks me

"Do you know the secret to living a long productive life?

I can proudly say

"Yes I know the secret because I've been with Lou Romano!"

Dad has it figured out; instinctively he just lives it, without trying to figure it out. Dad's a simple man and like he said before when asked about how do you do it, what's the secret to a productive long life?

Dad will say,

"I just like people I like to work and have something I like to do everyday, be happy, eat well, drink a little wine, and don't worry about anything simple as that!"

For the rest of my Golden years the Farm is in a living trust now and Joey and Elizabeth are set for their future. Where Sierra Valley Farms goes in the future is on its current course as long as I am fit to keep farming and as I say" I hope I have a few of Lou's genes!" My lifestyle is simple I plan on living out my years here on the farm and I already told Joey "When you put me out to greener pasture" you can spread my ashes over the tiki Bar at the pond and my life is complete.

About ten years ago being divorced and single all these years and with Joey so far not going into farming, I was worried that the farm would someday be sold and developed and that would end our legacy as farmers. So I sent a proposal to the Feather River Land Trust to purchase a conservation easement on my farm, to keep this property an organic farm in perpetuity. The Feather River Land Trust along with the Nature Conservancy has purchased over 30,000 acres in conservation easements with in Sierra Valley mainly for wildlife habitat and rangeland. Over the last five years they have purchased 2300 acres adjacent to my property and as of 2016 my proposal was accepted and finalized in 2019. Going into my Golden years I now can be at peace knowing that all the hard work and sacrifices that Grandpa Jacamo Folchi and his children made on this ranch (then) and the hard work and long hours and the perseverance that the Romano's put into this farm will be preserved as an organic farm for generations to come, well after I'm gone. Who knows, history may repeat itself and Joey may come back to farming, at least he will still have that option. For now, I'm still farming well into my Golden years!

Lou Romano

Dark Green

Farming into the Abyss

"If there is a future, it will be Green""

Petra Kelley

Using the abyss in the context of a farmer and his/her farm, an abyss is an immeasurable, bottomless pit that seems to have no end. It's a reoccurring nightmare in which the small farmer falls into an ever widening abyss between small farms versus the corporate Agribusiness, the mega- factory farms. What is the future for our young upcoming farmers who will replace us older farmers going into our Golden years? Farming into the abyss, what is in store for the future of our new farmers? Will there be an end to this abyss, this bottomless pit, or will it be a reoccurring nightmare for small farmers going against the overwhelming odds against them. Will the fate of David vs. Goliath ever come true?

Throughout the book I've selected the different colors of green to represent the different chapters of my life collimating into my Golden years. The color Green is pleasing and peaceful to all and lends itself to a wide array of experimentation and expression, as I've shown in each of my chapters. This is the one color of green that depicts the Abyss, the color of Dark Green. There's a dark side to every story, and to this story it is about the color of Dark Green representing the future of small farms and farming.

Dark green has a shade of resentment. Often the color used by wealthy businessmen, striving for more wealth, dark green signifies greed, the corporate agribusiness, and mega-factory farm model of scale, jealousy and the selfish desire, the feel of being slimy or "I've been slimed". Dark green is the color of money, and the military, a symbol of authority.

As a third generation farmer I've listened to and experienced the wisdom from my family ancestors, friends, farmers, and institutional colleagues. Throughout my 61 years of farming there has always been the pressure of the farming industry for farmers to "Get big or Get out!", but the little guy has always had an option to get big or to stay small and when I wrote *Why I Farm: Risking it all for a Life on the Land* there was the Green Revolution happening to mobilize young people to go into farming, a call to action about our food system. We had Michael Moore (Sicko), Michael Pollan (Omnivores Dilemma), Daniel Imhoff (Food Fight) and Joel Salatin (Food Inc.) along with others promoting organic food, buy local, support your family farmers and fighting against GMO (Genetically Modified organisms) foods, factory farming of animals, unhealthy processed foods and the condition of our health care system.

In 2011 it was the "Year of the Protester" according to *Time* Magazine. Where have we gone since, just adding more protesters to different causes without solutions? In 2012 I was writing about the loss of the small family farms, farmers getting older and less young people going into farming. It was a call to action for our banking institutions, government agencies and politicians to step up to the plate and help small farmers have access to land, get financial stability and access to credit and be able to have an "even-playing field" against the corporate Agribusiness, industrial factory farms. To regulate "Big Ag" to treat farm animals in humane ways with animal welfare laws, and keep the national organic standards high and true to its founders. The demonstrations in the streets then were the 99 percent main street working class was voicing their opposition to the *1* percent Wall Street, who were running the country.

Well I hate to tell you folks since 2011 and especially since the Trump Administration have taken over even though the consumer continues to care more about the food they eat and organic sales have risen, but things have gotten a lot worse, for small farmers. The total number of farms are on a steady decline; the average income of farmers have declined; the number of young people going into farming is in increasing, but the young farmers being able to sustain the farms are decreasing; and the average age of the farmer is 62 and getting older. We are entering uncertain times as to the direction of our food system. Who is going to grow our food in fifteen years when most of our current farmers are done with farming? Will we be importing all of our food in fifteen years if the young farmers can't take over farms? Is it the extinction of the Farmasaur? We are farming into an abyss, and can anybody stop it? I was looking over my past twenty five years of logs, ledgers, newspaper clippings and articles that I had collected and over those years there was a progression to "go green", create a healthier America. There was a lot of energy to create community gardens, improve school lunches with organic ingredients, and create new-farmer programs like Farm link and the Young Farmers Coalition. There was the "Buy local" movement with slogans everywhere, initiatives to require GMO's to be labeled and Obama care was passed to cover millions of Americans. For the first twenty years I've had a steady increase in people wanting my certified organic vegetables—my twenty seven shades of greens, chefs, farmers market customers, natural food stores, and CSA (community supported agriculture) members. But over the last five years I see this apathy, complacency, and this attitude "convenience is more important than substance" in the general public about their food choices, not only in the consumer but also in the chef's and local food stores, was it a "Fad" something that was cool for a while but now were on to something else that's "hip" and "in" right now..

Our attitudes as consumers, seems to follow the trends in technology and "convenience" seems to be the driving force for most consumers. There seems to be less loyalty by the consumers to support local small farms. Consumers today are "jumping ship" on small farmers and are supporting the Amazons of the world sacrificing locally grown, organic farm fresh and handmade products for commercialized, cheap made products from china, and unhealthy GMO tainted foods, for the convenience of home delivery. As small farmers we must continue to reinforce healthy and sustainable food resources, and strive to get more of our sustainable, organic foods into the consumer mainstream if we are to survive.

Going into this chapter I said to myself, "You know this is a very depressing way to look at this chapter talking about farming into the abyss and leave the reader with some uneasy feelings." "How can I spice it up a bit and keep it light-hearted and give some positive solutions?" The amazing part of the color green is that it depicts the positive and the negative and not only does green give you the feelings of inspiration, emotional wellbeing, trust, generosity of spirit, enlightenment, playfulness, offerings of peace and feelings of anticipation , but then you have its dark side; Dark green which represents deceit, selfishness, greed and abuse of power. The positive and the negative shades of green can be best seen in the fiction world of comics; green characters offset each other. You have the" good" side of green and the "bad" side of green which the color green is the color of most of our fictional characters. The villains and the superheroes are both green. There are actually twenty seven shades of cartoon characters too. What a coincident!!

Think about it, most of our famous villains have been associated with green, characters like: *The Green Goblin; The Grinch;* the *Creature of the Black Lagoon; Godzilla; The Mad Hatter; Doctor Doom; The Wicked Witch of the West; Frankenstein; Gremlins; Poison Ivy* and who could forget the slimiest of them all *"Slimer"* of the movie

Ghostbusters! The color green most times has positive connotations we have our "Green Good Guys" too or superheroes that come to save the day like: *The Incredible Hulk; She-Hulk; The Green Hornet; Swamp Thing; Jolly Green Giant; Teenage Mutant Ninja Turtles; Gomorra;* and who could forget the master, *Yoda*.

To lighten up the discussion in this chapter about Farming into the Abyss, I've chosen to structure the discussion basically being the big government and big agribusiness are the villains (which they are); and small family farms, young new farmers, organic food (health), and environment are the super heroes. I've divided up my group of villains against my group of super heroes so please enjoy a very dark green discussion.

It's just so appropriate and fitting that most of the villain characters that I will be talking about are "slime-ball" characters that I will identify according to our fictional characters for instance: President Trump was a tough one because he's a cross between *"Slimer"* a Ghostbusters character, a foul smelling, vapor green blob ghost, with an orange-hair comb-over, known for a big appetite for McDonalds hamburgers, and leaves behind slime where ever he goes or the *"Green Goblin "* Spiderman's archenemy, a narcissist evil supervillain, disguised as the President of the U.S., who took a serum that drove him totally insane, and flies around the country on a glider hurling bombs disguised as pumpkins to create havoc in Washington D.C. and the World. So I think because President Trump is definitely both characters, I'm going to combine them and call Trump *"The Slimy-Green Goblin"* to represent him in this chapter.

Another notable group of villains will be *Slimy-Green Goblins* Administration, they will be referred to as *"The Creatures of the Black Lagoon"* a terrifying group of green, reptile-like, gill-man creatures from the murky depths of the abyss that reap havoc on the small farmer, migrant workers and supports anything the *Slimy-Green Goblin* recommends.

Next will be the USDA; they will be referred to as *the "Green-Eyed Monster"* a hypothetical green-eyed monster that rears its ugly head up every four years (Farm Bill) and attacks and bites small farmers. The Green-Eyed Monster has a sidekick that speaks for him. Secretary of Agriculture who I will call *"Gumby"*, because the fictional character of Gumby is a soft-spineless piece of green clay that can be molded into anything the Green-Eyed Monster wants him to be.

The other agency that has been infiltrated by "Slime balls" is the Environmental Protection Agency (EPA). The *Slimy-Green Goblin* has appointed a number of agrichemical executives to the staff and that have wanted to abolish the EPA for years. So the villain I've chosen for the EPA is *"Frankenstein."*

This villain is considered to be the worst supervillain of all time by many small farmers and that is Agribusiness(Agrifood, Agrichemical) Mega-Factory Farms which will be called *Dr. Doom* the archenemy of the Fantastic Four (Land, Food, Water and Air)the villain that has psychic powers as well as the ability casting bolts of energy to take over farms. They have mystic abilities and genius uses in genetically modified organisms (GMO); biochemistry; cybernetics and with the biggest lobbying group in Washington D.C. *Dr. Doom* is a sly deceiver of the American public and public enemy number one to the small family farms.

The last villain is the *Grinch*. We all know about the Grinch and how he stole Christmas, taking away all the presents from all the girls and boys creating the "boo-hoo" in Whoville. Well there's no one that can represent the Grinch better than the GOP group of Republican Congressman and Senators. This group will be called the *Grinches*. The group of "haters' with shriveled hearts "two-sizes too small", that take away health care, take from the poor and give to the rich, and discriminate against race, LBGT, immigrants and support white supremacy.

For my super heroes who are going to save American agriculture and small family farms there are only a few who can take on these villains. My first super hero is the *"Jolly Green Giant"*, a fictional character, from a canned peas advertisement, tall and casting a shadow from a strong body built of healthy, organic vegetables, famous for his slogan…"ho…ho…ho…the green giant" represents the small family farms (farmers).

My next super hero is the *"Teenage Mutant Ninja Turtles"*, who represent the Millennials, young farmers trained in organic farming, coming from the inner cities and the suburbs to battle *Dr. Doom* today and in the future while being forgotten in American agriculture and hidden from society. They are the future of American agriculture.

My greatest super hero is someone that can protect and represent the environment! He has to protect us from the evils that try to destroy the environment (Land, Water, Air), and the forces of global climate change. This super hero is *"Swamp Thing"* a fictional comic character in the 1970's that is a humanoid made up of vegetation that lives in the swamp and fights to protect humanity and the environment against terrorist acts and supernatural threats (environmental groups like Eco Watch, Sierra Club etc.). This fictional character is going to "drain the swamp!" Gee…I've heard that phrase before?

Last but not least we need a wise master, a superhero that has compassion and believes in the good of all mankind. This *"Yoda"* will represent President Barack Obama who may not have been perfect but had the compassion and believed in the good of mankind, and our Farming mentors like Wendell Berry and others.

We are in uncertain times right now, especially with the *Slimy-Green Goblin* (Trump), and his *Creatures from the Black Lagoon*(Trump administration), in charge. First thing the *Slimy-Green Goblin* is doing is rolling back anything *Yoda*(Obama) did in his administration whether it was right or wrong, so you first take that into account. We have fallen back over fifty years on our civil rights, the *Grinches* (GOP-Congress) are back to their old ways of hate and bigotry, there is obvious division in this country, women's rights have to be substantiated again, more negativity and "gloom and doom" than I've ever witnessed in my lifetime. We have fallen back 100 years in dealing with immigration. The *Slimy-Green Goblin and his Creatures of the Black Lagoon* along with the *Grinches* are treating immigrants like they did at the turn of the 20th Century, like dirt and without any rights. Are we going create *"Slimy-Green Goblin* Island" (like Ellis Island) and send the immigrants through the same embarrassing ordeal as we did in the early 1900's? What is happening to the wonderful USA? We are now being hated around the world more now than ever with *the Slimy-Green Goblin* and his *Creatures from the Black Lagoon.*

It's all about the rich, and when you're (farmers) at the bottom of the totem pole and one of the least desirable and lowest income occupations in America, the "shit flows downhill!" Farmers what we are faced with going into 2019, is that we're pretty much on our own again.

Green-Eyed Monster (USDA Agriculture and the Farm Bill)

Well the *Green-eyed Monster* is going to rear its ugly head once again! The outlook for agriculture going into 2019 is not bright for the *Jolly Green Giant* (Small Farmers); it's great for *Dr. Doom*(Agribusiness) that controls most of the food produced in America.

Dr. Doom controls:

- 85% of the beef market.
- 75% of the sow (pork) market.
- Over 50% of the poultry market.

It all starts at the top with the *Slimy-Green Goblin* and his *Creatures of the Black Lagoon* dictating the direction of Agriculture. Politico reports that 22 of the 42 appointees by the *Slimy-Green Goblin* (Trump) to the *Green-Eyed Monster*(USDA)had some kind of involvement in the *Slimy-Green Goblin's* campaign and very few have any agriculture experience. That will give you some idea of what to expect in the coming years.

In summary according to the *Green-Eyed Monsters'* Census Bureau and the Department of Agriculture their focus is shifting from supporting the *Jolly Green Giant* (Small Farmers) to supporting *Dr. Doom*(Agribusiness). Over the past farm bill, the number of large farms with sales over $500,000 annually increased significantly, while those farms with sales under $350,000 annually, decreased, losing over 8,000 farms in 2016.

In the big picture:

- 90% of all farms in America have annual sales of less than $350,000
- 80% of those had annual sales less than $100,000
- 50% (family farms) had less than $10,000 in agriculture sales.

The sliding scale is not moving in the small farmers favor. *Dr. Doom* (3.2% of all farms), produces over 50% of the food in America, and the largest (8% of all farms) farms grows most of the food in America. *Dr. Doom* gets all the incentives, tax breaks, crop insurance, and lobbying power in Washington D.C. The *Jolly Green Giant* (Small Farmer) is forgotten.

The *Green-Eyed Monster's* (USDA) definition of a family farm is that he associates almost every farm as a "Family farm", it doesn't matter how big the farm is, but its only stipulation is that the farm has some sort of "ownership" by a family member. The family member must have 51% assets of that farm, and being corporate has no bearing on the classification of a family farm. Corporate status or non-family farm has an absentee ownership, hired managers and are the large corporate, agribusiness, and mega factory farms like Tyson, Cargill, and JBS Swift etc. A corporate farm is basically classified that it has no family ownership. So under they're classification 90% of all farms are family farms and they can brag and say that most of America is run by family farmers, even though 85% of these farms make over five million dollars a year. The *Green-Eyed Monster* says "Look we're doing a great job of supporting family farmers", even though we only have less than 30% of the farms we had in the 1930's.

The *Green-Eyed Monster* is all about agricultural productivity, the bigger the farm, the more efficient, the more productivity. That's it... bottom line! It's all about *Dr. Doom* efficiently growing commodities of wheat; rice; corn, cotton, soybean, beef, sow (pork), dairy, and poultry. In 1996 forty six percent of all farms had annual sales of less than $350,000 and by 2016 these farms only account for twenty six percent. The mid-sized farms have consolidated into big farms or have been bought out by mega farms to make them even bigger and to reduce competition. The *Green-Eyed Monster* sends out an annual agricultural survey that's mandatory for all of us agricultural producers to complete, (mine is sitting on my desk as we speak), to over 1.7 million of us. Over the last four years we have lost over a million acres in crop land down to 911 million acres. Even though the total acres are decreasing the acreages of each farm are getting larger, which suggests the theory that small farms are going out of business while the larger farms are consolidating and getting larger.

The *Green-Eyed Monsters'* (USDA) 2016 census shows:

- There has been a huge increase in farms over 2,000 acres
- No increase in mid-sized farms (450-2,000 acres)
- A loss of 8000 family farms less than 400 acres
- In 1996 there were over 217 million farms
- 2016 we are down to a little over 2.06 million farms and seeing a steady decline annually.

So what does the *Green-Eyed Monster* see in the *Jolly Green Giants* future? According to his definition of a family farm (which about 85% are corporate farms), he predicts that the *Jolly Green Giant* (Small Farmers)will still dominate the statistics but will have to adapt to new technologies i.e. robots and drones, GPS, and driverless tractors, genetics (GMO), and the priorities will be for the larger farms. The *Jolly Green Giant*, which accounts for only six percent of all jobs in American and the bulk of small farmers income is earned off the farm, will again be left to fend for themselves.

The history of the Farm Bill has always been about giving the subsidies to the mega commodity farmers of wheat, rice, corn, soybean, dairy farmers, beef and pork industry. The small farmer must be creative in our local communities to build relationships with residences by way of community gardens, corner farmers markets and establishing local food hubs to distribute local fruits and vegetables. Remember cash is king for the small farmers. It's so important to keep our local dollars local!

The Farm Bill has just been approved for 2019, so what can we expect from the *Slimy-Green Goblin (Trump)* and his *Creatures from the Black Lagoon*(Trump Administration)? Well to quote Michael Pollan in an interview on Robert Reich's "In Conversation" The *Slimy Green Goblin* has dumped the *Jolly Green Giant*!" Yes the *Jolly Green Giant* has been "Slimed", and the red states who believed the *Slimy-Green Goblin* and who voted for him, along with most farmers…well…another promise broken!

The *Slimy-Green Goblin* first claims that his *Creatures from the Black Lagoon* and the Grinches (GOP-Congress)are "fighting for our farmers and our rural communities" then he goes ahead and states to his Secretary of Agriculture that he plans on cutting the *Green-Eyed Monsters'*(USDA) budget by at least twenty one percent. Civil Eats reports that these cuts would cause the closure or rural offices that provide support to farmers; cut funds for conservation programs which work with farmers to help soil and water quality for plant and animal health In addition it would eliminate supporting rural business and job training. Really looks like he's "fighting for our farmers and rural communities" all right!

The *Slimy-Green Goblin* made it clear that small farmers and rural communities are not a top priority for him and his *Creatures from the Black Lagoon*. The *Slimy-Green Goblin's* other projected budget cuts include $900 million from the health education fund and $145 million from the (SNAP) Federal Food Stamp program that promotes healthy eating habit to help prevent obesity, like providing cooking demonstrations for farmers markets. Along with SNAP, another program to be removed would be the (FMPP) the Farmers Market Promotion Program, according to the agency. The FMPP has helped more than double the number of farmers markets since being established in the 2008 Farm Bill. Farmers market have grown from 3,000 to over 8,600 markets in 2016, and its worth in the program is over $58 million. Farmers markets sell around $3 billion in food and bring sustainable foods and farming into our local communities. This is a major blow to the *Jolly Green* Giant (Small Farmers) and rural communities.

Currently according to Senator John Tester of Montana, the *Slimy-Green Goblin* and his *Creatures of the Black Lagoon* have rescinded *Yoda's* (Obama) 2016 Fair Market Value Bill that impacts the Grain Inspection, Packers, and Stockyards Administration's ability to enforce rules so that *Dr.* Doom (Agribusiness)can't take advantage of the *Jolly Green Giant*. This rule was put in place by *Yoda in 2016* just to do that, to have USDA protect the *Jolly Green Giant* from *Dr. Doom.*

Senator Tester stated that under the old rule if the *Dr. Doom's* packers did harm to the *Jolly Green Giant* they could take them to court for damages, now that the *Slimy-Green Giant* has thrown out the rule and now the *Jolly Green Giant* would have to prove that *Dr. Doom* had done harm to the entire U.S. industry and that's hard to prove, matter of fact not going to happen. So now *Dr. Doom* (Agribusiness) can do anything he wants to the *Jolly Green Giant* (Small Farmers), with little to no recourse from him. Again *Dr. Doom* can now crush the *Jolly Green Giant*. Without the Fair Market Rule, Senator Tester says, "If the small farmers can't get fair market value for their products most of us are going to go broke pretty quick, I can tell you." Tester continues to say "That's why we've seen so much consolidation and see rural communities drying up." That's why this Fair Market Rule that's been thrown out is a prime example of *Dr.* Doom(Agribusiness)being able to take advantage of the *Jolly Green Giant*(Small Farmers) Senator Tester concludes with "the rule was set up in 2016 to protect the little guy. Throwing it out goes against the foundation of this country to support family farms and ranchers."

Again, small family ranchers and farmers have to diverse their farms and ranches to utilize vegetable, fruit and animal operations as to not put all their eggs in one basket. Price setting is very common in the larger wholesale markets of produce and livestock, farmers must avoid being caught up in those markets where your hands are tied.

In addition other programs that will affect agriculture are reducing regulations of animal welfare on factory farms; the Clean water Act (WOTUS); food safety initiatives; and GMO labeling requirements. Consider the *Slimy-Green Goblins'*(Trump) new tax bill that was passed by the *Grinches*(GOP-Congress), according to Civil Eats, economists from the *Green-Eyed Monster*(USDA) estimate that the new tax law will raise the burden on earning for the lowest 20% of family farms. The richest 10% will capture 50-70% of the benefits. As far as the estate tax the vast majority of farmers are no way impacted by the estate tax. Even before the new tax law in 2017, only 80 farms were affected. There will also be more "give-a-ways", so called subsides (crop insurance) for *Dr. Doom*. Again this shows that the *Slimy-Green Goblin's* priorities are not with the *Jolly Green Giant* and rural communities, but for the rich, and the wealthiest of farms.

The *Jolly Green Giant* is wading in unchartered waters right now slowly sinking into the abyss. It is pretty evident what the priority of the *Slimy-Green Goblin* and his *Creatures from the Black Lagoon* and the *Green-Eyed Monster* are heading, and that's to support *Dr. Doom*. The *Jolly Green Giant* is really going to have to find his/her niche and diversify his/her farming operations within our local communities to survive.

Dr. Doom (Agribusiness, Mega Factory Farms, Deregulation)

The *Slimy-Green Goblin* (Trump) signed an executive order "Promoting Agriculture and Prosperity in Rural America" in April of 2017. He said " I'm directing *Gumby*(Secretary of Agriculture, USDA) to work with other members of my cabinet to identify and eliminate unnecessary regulation that hurt our nations farmers and rural communities", he told fourteen Agribusiness executives, like the American Farm Bureau, Syngenta, Cargill, Tyson to name a few, assembled for the event.

In Eric-Holt-Gimenez's book: *A Foodies Guide to Capitalism*, and the director of *Food First; Gimenez* states that; *Gumby*, wants to help monopolize the Agrifoods corporations to squeeze profits from farmers and consumers. We can expect the further disappearance of small to mid-sized farms and further corporate concentration of our food system under the *Slimy-Green Goblin* and his *Creatures from the Black Lagoon*.

Dr. Doom wants to create a monopoly and reduce competition within the industry that causes individual participants like the *Jolly Green Giant* to become price takers with no control over the prices they are paid or the way they raise their animals. *Dr. Doom* keeps "squeezing" the mid-size farmers more and more to the point that they either have to go out of business or sell out to the mega-factory farms that then get larger and larger. Pretty soon you will only have a few companies raising all the meat and produce in the U.S. and not only dictating the farmers prices and how and what animals they are to raise, or crops they grow, but also dictating to the consumer what meat or produce they will be eating because the consumer may only have a few choices to choose from in the corporate agribusiness model.

Civil eats reports that we can expect the further hollowing out of the American Heartland and a worsening of the social strife, food insecurity, and increased opioid addictions currently devastating our country. Somehow we need to break the stranglehold on our food, put people back to the land, invest in our local, rural communities and get anti-trust laws in place to break up the monopolies, and stop speculating with our farmland and food.

They are correct and it's up to our local communities and governments to offer incentives to young people to become farmers by offering affordable land, low or no interest loans and grants to beginning and existing farmers for initial start-up and expanding operations. All communities should provide vocational training and farm certification programs through their local colleges to encourage farming and provide for the training and internships on existing farms and community gardens in urban and suburban areas where there exists food deserts.

One of the biggest threats to our small farmers and consumers is the threat of deregulation by the *Slimy-Green Monster* and his *Creatures from the Black Lagoon*. He and his cronies have focused on reversing all the regulation set in place by *Yoda* (Obama), no matter whether they were good or bad, most were based on scientific research justifying the regulation to be put in place. The *Slimy-Green Goblin* and his goons *The Creatures of the Black Lagoon* plan on deregulating as many as possible to help the wealthiest corporations in America.

First the *Slimy-Green* Goblin (Trump) has rolled back the animal welfare regulations for *Dr. Dooms'*(Agribusiness) factory farms, mega-dairies, fed lots, and poultry. According to Civil Eats mega dairies have moved into Oregon, along the Columbia River and with the deregulation of waste and air emissions are causing pollution to the region. *Dr. Dooms'* mega dairies, feed lots, and poultry factory farms plants deposit millions of acres of animal waste every year. Lagoons of up to 20 acres in size are set up to handle the waste. Leaks in these lagoons have polluted the ground water (drinking water) and have killed thousands of fish in the river ways. At that time, about twelve years ago there were no restriction on air emissions and no regulations for restricting or monitoring nitrates getting into the groundwater.

Ten years ago a Oregon Dairy Air Quality task force was set up to review emissions of air pollutants (ammonia, hydrogen sulfide, methane, nitrogen oxides and particulate matter) with recommendations for the State and Federal officials so they could set up some rules for air quality. Ten years later none of the recommendations went anywhere despite the fact that it was a consensus list of recommendations. To make matters even worse, the *Slimy -Green Goblin* (Trump) and his *Creatures of the Black* Lagoon (Trump Administration)have deregulated the animal welfare restrictions for organic production so now the animals that the consumer thought were raised in human ways (free- range, outside with some space, not penned in stepping on each other) can be more concentrated similar to a conventional factory farm and can produce even more waste per acre. *Dr. Doom* has once again deceived the consumer. Please *Swamp Thing* (Environmental Groups), come and save the day!

Comparing factory farms is like any extractive industry like mining or timber. It's the same model but with a different face. *Dr. Doom* comes in to a community and calls himself the *Jolly Green Giant,* and then they extract all the water, the local wealth and basically leave you all the "shit!" "You can put lipstick on a cow but it's still *Dr. Doom's cow!"* What happens most times in these rural communities *Dr. Doom* will come into these small towns disguised as the *Jolly Green Giant,* and flood the markets with cheap milk, beef, poultry etc. and put the small farmers out of business. In this scenario in Oregon, *Dr. Doom's* dairy put nine small dairies out of business while polluting the community's drinking water and river ways. Thank god for *Swamp Thing* (Environmental Groups) to come in and rally the community against the pollution.

Instead of having *Dr. Doom,* if they would have kept these nine dairies in business within the community these dairies (farms) the people working and owning these farms put wealth back into the community they live. They create local jobs, spending their money in the local community by frequenting the hardware store and auto shop stores for parts, utilize local mechanic shops; and their kids go to local schools, churches and social, community events. When *Dr. Doom* moves into a local community they take away those local jobs, bring in low wage workers from outside the community and all of their purchases go through a purchasing agent from out-of-state that bulk orders by bids, and ships the materials and supplies needed right to the factory farm. All the profits from *Dr. Doom* go directly to the corporate office then on to the executives and the shareholders, with nothing rolled back into the community they take over.

In 2015 Yoda (Obama) enacted regulations in the Clean Water Act – WOTUS (Water of the United States) which were responsible for cleaning up rivers and placed 117 million people's drinking water under the program, which accounted for a third of the U.S. population. One of the first deregulation orders from the *Slimy-Green Goblin* (Trump) and *Frankenstein* (EPA) was to get rid of the *Swamp Thing* (Environmental Laws). The *Slimy-Green Goblin* called WOTUS "the worst example of federal regulation." *Dr. Dooms* (Agribusiness) boss the American Farm Bureau (which is made up of all Agribusiness and Agrichemical and insurance executives) was excited about rolling back all these regulation to get rid of the *Swamp Thing* (Environmental Laws). The Farm Bureau fully supports to rescind this rule, thus again jeopardizing our drinking water and river ways.

Over the years small farmers and ranchers have been the best stewards of the land. Utilizing organic and biodynamic practices on small farms and ranches small farms reduce the runoff of nitrates from fertilizers and animal waste from entering our waterways. Crop rotation and diversity of crops helps the environment by way strengthening soil structure and health and prevents erosion of our soils. These large mono-crop systems and mega factory animal farms are ruining our waterways and were losing thousands of tons of our soil each year to erosion.

The other disturbing roll back of regulations is dealing with *Frankenstein* (EPA) itself. It's pretty common knowledge that *Frankenstein* is made up of executives from *Dr. Doom's* office. As the *Swamp Thing* (Environmental Defense Fund) said it best, The EPA is increasingly dominated by people who spent decades fighting to block safeguards, undermining science, and lobbying for the polluters." This agency is led by ex-Agribusiness executives, appointed by the *Slimy-Green Goblin,* who have spent a lifetime in litigation against the EPA over regulations and who have said publicly that if it was up to them they would abolish the EPA department. Well there you go *Swamp Thing* (Environment) you'll need all your super powers to handle *Frankenstein* (EPA)!

The *Slimy-Green Goblin and Frankenstein* have shown no interest in helping to protect *Swamp Thing.* They are attacking anything that protects the environment. Opening up offshore oil drilling in Alaska, gutting the Clean Water Act, open mining in our national parks, allowing trophy hunting of endangered exotic animals, and allowing previously banned harmful pesticides to be used on our food. They are rescinding all the protections so that *Dr. Doom* can maximize profits, at the expense of the environment and our children's future. Its pure greed, capitalism at its worst!

Air pollution is a major contributor to asthma and premature death. Lisa Garcia a columnist states that a 2014 study found that low income and people of color live in communities with 38% more nitrogen dioxide, a compound that is a precursor to smog. The nation has made strides in reducing this type of pollution when *Frankenstein* (EPA) was under the control of *Yoda,* who set protective smog standards in 2015. After *Yoda* (Obama), in October of 2017, *Frankenstein* (EPA) was required to pinpoint those areas of the country that weren't meeting the 2015 air standards. But instead *Frankenstein* ignored federal law by missing the October deadline and furthermore has extended numerous deadlines delaying action on other regulations.

The fact is we must replace these irresponsible politicians with responsible members who can protect the environment. If our farming and ranching practices are part of the problem we must reverse the impacts that they are causing to the environment. Farmers must demand that these regulations stay in place to protect the farmer, the consumer and the environment. They all work together to help protect food safety in America.

At the end of October 2017 *Frankenstein* issued a directive barring scientists who receive federal grants from serving on science advisory committees, in addition he began replacing them with people that have a tract record of disagreeing with established scientific research and have financial connections with *Dr. Doom*(Agribusiness). One of his appointees actually claims that air pollution is good for children. He states that the "modern air is a little too clean for optimum health." Michael Honeycutt the head toxicologist at the Texas Commission on Environmental Quality agency doubts that smog affects asthma and says "The quality of your air and water, and your exposure to toxic and hazardous substances—is determined to a great extent by your race and income." Well that says it all! In other words if you live in the low income-inner cities or poor suburbs you're pretty much out of luck, "up a creek without a paddle."!

Frankenstein (EPA) has now sued a number of *Swamp Things* (Environmental Groups) cohorts including the American Lung Association, the National Parks Association and the Environmental Defense Fund over many of these regulations. This is one example of how the *Slimy-Green Goblin* and his *Creatures of the Black Lagoon* have supported *Frankenstein and Dr. Doom* by stalling the implementation of required health and environmental protections so that *Dr. Doom* (Agribusiness) can focus on their bottom lines rather than the communities or neighborhoods they may be polluting and avoiding *Swamp Thing* (Environment and Environmental Groups)!

Frankenstein (EPA) also rescinded *Yoda's* Clean Power Plan which would have reduced emissions, a primary driver of climate change, in which the *Slimy-Green Goblin* has taken the United States out of the Paris Agreement. The United Nations framework convention on climate change (UNFCCC) and we are the only country (U.S.) in the world that does not support climate change, dismissing the overwhelming scientific evidence that fuel emissions and pollution affect climate change and its threat to *Swamp Thing* and the world's climates.

As if this isn't enough bad news for the *Jolly Green Giant and Swamp Thing ... the beat goes on...*in the world of pesticide regulations according to *Swamp Thing* (Eco Watch) *Frankenstein*(EPA) is considering allowing a Bee killing pesticide (thiamethoxam) to be sprayed on 165 million acres of *Dr. Doom's* wheat, barley, corn, sorghum, alfalfa, rice, and potato crops. This pesticide has the potential to cause catastrophic losses to bees, birds and aquatic invertebrates. Despite the known dangers, the *Slimy-Green Goblin and Frankenstein* seem again to avoid *Swamp Thing* and ignore the risks to the environment.

While we are on the abuse of pesticide regulations, lets' look at a case in California that in 2015 *Yoda* announced it would ban neurotoxic insecticides (chlorpyrifos) on food crops. After *Yoda, Frankenstein* announced it would not allow the ban after all the scientific studies has shown overwhelming evidence that it affects children's neurological development, and is detrimental to *Swamp Thing* (Environment). It is one of the most used pesticides around schools in fifteen agricultural counties in California determined by the California Department of Health in 2015. The study show that the pesticide levels around these schools were 3-44 times the acceptable level limits. California is working with *Swamp Thing* and proposed to supersede *Frankenstein* and ban it. California has the right to do that as well. Thank God that I live in California!

This should be a wake-up call to all Americans that we cannot just be complacent about these issues. We must protect the environment and our food system for our children and futures to come. It all begins with our Food system. We must protect and enhance our local food systems from these mega farms who spray pesticides wildly with no consequences for their actions.

Many times it's not only the big government that small farmers are up against, but it's what big agriculture does behind closed doors lobbying, and pressuring our politicians and government officials to sway in big agricultures favor. That is the case with our organic standards. The integrity of the organic standards is in jeopardy. The Hill reports that the interests of *Dr. Doom* are having an outsized and growing influence on the organic standards compared to the waning influence of organic farmers, who started the movement. Organic food is becoming a $50 billion business and *Dr. Doom* wants to change the rules.

How? Many of the concentrated Animal feeding operations (CAFO) are over cramming animals into building without access to the outdoors which is against the organic standards for animal welfare. There are dairy (CAFO) with over 15,000 cows crammed in a desert feedlot that are not meeting the organic standards for grazing. There is total corrupting in the *Green-Eyed Monsters* (USDA) inspectors that are not doing surprise inspections as they are required to do under the National Organic Program (NOP). These corrupt inspectors actually will contact the CAFO beforehand to tell them he/she are coming out to inspect so that the CAFO can release the livestock for that day to pass the inspection then go back to cramming them into their defined spaces. It won't be a problem anymore because as of December the *Slimy-Green Goblin* (Trump) has now removed the requirements of these organic standards.

A rapidly growing percentage of fruits and vegetables labeled "organic" on the grocery shelves are being produced hydroponically, without soil, and in huge-industrial scale facilities according to the *Green-Eyed Monster's* task force. Hydroponics has become a huge industry and to become "organic" will revolutionize the production of fruits and vegetables and take over the organic fruit and vegetable market. The consumer will no longer know what was grown in the soil as "true" organic or what was grown in liquid-chemical solution "fake" organic.

The Hill reports that the NOSB (National Organic Standards Board), in November 2017 approved hydroponic production of a 100 percent "non-organic" liquid feeding program and considers it now an organic process even though the produce is not grown in soil. The NOSB responded favorably to a massive lobbying effort on the part of *Dr. Doom* (Agribusiness) and voted 8-7 to reject an attempt by the sustainable "true "organic farmers to prevent hydroponic produce from being organic. Many organic farmers insist that the decision is "illegal" under the Organic Food Production Act (OFPA). Chapman said "Five years ago the organic system was working pretty well. There were no issues with the organic standards." There was a challenge to the NOSB in 2010, when a Mexican hydroponic company proposed hydropon- ics to the Board but was unanimously rejected for organic production the organic label is at risk. There is growing pressure from *Dr. Doom* to weaken the organic standards in order to increase profits at the ex- pense of traditional organic practices (grown in soil)established by the originating organic boards and committees. It is incumbent on organic farmers and consumers to work together to maintain the integrity of organic food and be vigilant and active against the efforts of *Dr. Doom* to put profits over integrity. Farmer Dave Chapman quoted "Organic farmers will have no choice but to leave the program if we want to of- fer a real alternative to industrial agriculture." *The Green-Eyed Monster* (USDA) should not be in charge of defining organic. We must be aware of "fake Organic" it's all around us now and once again the American public has been deceived by *Dr. Doom* (Agribusiness)!

A fool proof system for the consumer is again is not to trust commer- cial advertising and false advertising of organic products. I buy organic produce and products from my local farmers and farmers markets. I get to know my farmers, even visit their farms. They love to brag about how they grow your food. That is the best way to know what you are putting into your body and your children's bodies. Support your local food Coop's and food hubs they know how their farmers farm...and remember buy organic whenever possible. We small organic farmers are inspected annually and can only use organic products and practices on our farm. Conventional mega farms can spray whatever they want on your fruits and vegetables without telling you anything on the label. The labeling laws a flawed and need to be changed drastically!

We small farmers are facing difficult years ahead of us farming into this abyss that seems to have no light at the end of the tunnel, We must continue our farming journey on our own and it's up to us older farmers to pass on our wisdom to the upcoming "greenhorns", whom I've named the *"Teenage Mutant Ninja Turtles"*(Young, millennial farmers) who must take on the challenges that lies ahead of them to confront the farming evils , the likes of the *Slimy-Green* Goblin(Trump); *Creatures from the Black Lagoon*(Trump Administration), the *Green-Eyed Monster*(USDA), *and Frankenstein*(EPA).

Teenage Mutant Ninja Turtles (Young Farmers and Millennials)

Still farming after all these years may be a forgotten slogan for the Millennials. Young and old farmers face a daunting list of challenges and ominous forces against them in the upcoming years. The *Teenage Mutant Ninja Turtles* have an agenda, and the energy to overcome the barriers to their success in agriculture, including access to land, affordable health care, Labor, and mounting student debt, but success will require deliberate policy change at all levels of government.

A survey conducted by the National Young Farmers Coalition (NYFC) in 2016 with 94 different partner organizations collected data from over 3500 current, former, and aspiring U.S. Farmers under 40 years of age. The top challenge is land access, finding affordable land on a farm income. It is also the main reason why farmers quit farming and why aspiring farmers haven't yet started.

According to *The Green-Eyed Monsters* (USDA) survey in 2016

- 40 percent of the small to mid-size farms made a profit
- The average income of those farms was $56,000 per farm
- 2007 the average income had dropped to $26,000 per year
- 2012 the percentage of farmers turning a profit had not changed, but the average income continued to drop.
- 2013 the net farm income for U.S. Farmers has declined 50% percent
- The median farm income for 2017 has dropped another $1,325

As far as government subsidies to farmers, farm subsidies account for:

- 3-5% percent of *the Green-Eyed Monsters* (USDA) budget
- 60% of all farmers receive no subsidies (that's all the small and mid-sized farms, plus specialty crops like fruits and vegetable growers).
- The top 1% of the farms receives 20% of the subsidies
- The top 15% receive 50% of the subsidies

So basically *Dr. Doom* (Agribusiness, Mega Farms) gets all of the subsidies. So the *Teenage Mutant Ninja Turtles* (Young, millennial farmers) are facing incredible odds against them. Can they successfully take over farms from our aging farmers?

To start, the Farm Bill has to be changed, the subsidies that were put in place by Roosevelt in the 1930's provided protection to the farmers of that era. Times have drastically changed and the large mega farms and factories don't need the subsidies to compete with the world markets. Trump's tariffs alone are causing more problems for American farmers than competing in the global marketplace. The subsidies need to be differed to all fruit and vegetable growers grossing less than one million dollars. All young and existing farmers grossing less than $250,000 should be tax exempt, and all farm loans of less than one million dollars should be less than 4% . Collateral loans must be reinstated and grants of up to $100,000 should be available to all small family farms grossing less than $500,000. The priorities of the funding should be to enhance local distribution of local foods produced by local communities. There has to be incentives set forth to encourage young people to go into farming.

According to the NYFC agriculture in the U.S. is at a breaking point. Farmers over 65 outnumber farmers under 35 by a margin of six to one, and U.S. farmland is overwhelmingly concentrated in the hands of the older farmers. Nearly two-thirds of farmland is managed by someone over 55. The National Agricultural Statistic Service estimates that over the next five years nearly 100 million acres will change ownership and will need a new farmer.

A lot of these new farmers are second generation farmers that are taking over, and many had ran from the farm (like I did) then due to different situations that happen later in life (divorce, death, finances etc.) they return to the farm later in Life. Clara Coleman, the daughter of the famous organic farmer, Elliot Coleman says "Dad's success at first wasn't enough to entice me to follow his footsteps." "I spent most of my life trying to get away from farming." When she was young farming "wasn't sexy enough."

Civil Eats reports that around the country second generation farmers like Clara Coleman are significant on that they become a bridge between the brutal first steps of a farm, and its potential wonder years—the years when farm debt, is relieved, the equipment paid for, and the systems and markets established. But second generations still have strong hesitations about becoming farmers themselves, even coming from successful farms. "It's a significant challenge" says Jerry Cosgrove, director of the Farm Legacy Program at American Farm Land Trust (AFT. "The assets themselves are valuable, but it can also be an interpersonal challenge; in many cases you're not just transferring assets, but a business as well as a lifestyle—and when people live on a farm, it's also a residence."

Farm numbers have been in a steady decline since the 1980's suggesting many children of the back-to-the-landers left the farm when they had an opportunity to get better jobs in the city or go off to college. Farming is an extremely difficult, uncertain way of life. Farming is rewarding, noble way of life, but it isn't for everyone. There are clear benefits from taking over a farm, especially an organic farm. Although stress and depression are common among farmers, as are injury and divorce (33%). One study suggests that organic farmers identify feeling happy more often than conventional farmers. The value of transferring to a second generation farmer is the partnership and bond between the incoming farmer and the older farmer. Old farmers still want to work and contribute to the farm in their golden years (Look at Lou Romano!). They want to still drive tractor and tinker around the farm. They pass the "reins" over to the younger farmer now and they get to do what they want to do on the farm not because the "have to" but now because the "want to!"

Dr. Merriman (NYFC) said that "America desperately needs people to repopulate our farm and ranch lands. If nothing more is done to help transition young people into American agriculture we will be importing all our foods." Fortunately many young Americans are stepping up and launching new farm businesses. The 2012 census report showed an increase of farmers over the previous census, in the number of farmers under 35 years of age. But also shows a decrease in farmers between the ages of 35 to 44. Speculation is that these new farmers are unable to sustain the farms over time due to capital financing needs, and long term debts. Farmers are winning a few battles but losing the War against *Dr. Doom* (Agribusiness, Mega Farms).

The *Teenage Mutant Ninja Turtles* (Young, millennial farmers) are seriously dedicated to environmental stewardship with 25% describing their practices as "sustainable", and 63% describing as organic. They are highly educated millennials and racially diverse with 63% had high optimism that they are making or eventually making sufficient income to meet their life goals.

Land Access was the top challenge for the *Teenage Mutant Ninja Turtles* without secure land tenure farmers are unable to invest in on-farm infrastructures and conservation practices critical to soil and water quality, financial equity and their businesses. According to the *Green-Eyed Monster* (USDA) land values in agriculture real estate doubled between the years 2004-2013. Particularly around our nation's cities—whose access to markets, make land desirable for working farmers. The NYFC states that development pressure, high demand from other farms, and speculation and competition from non-farm entities has made land prohibitively expensive for the *Teenage Mutant Ninja Turtles*. The *Jolly Green Giant* (Small Farmers) can't compete with land developers who have access to cash and credit institutions, not available to the *Jolly Green Giant* and the *Teenage Ninja Turtles*.

Student loan debt is cited by the *Teenage Mutant Ninja Turtles* as very significant to their success in starting a farm business, or preventing them from succeeding in agriculture. In a 2014 survey by the NYFC respondents had an average of $35,000 in student loan debt. Fifty three percent of them were farming but struggled to make monthly loan payments. Thirty percent were not farming, or had to delay farming and got jobs away from farming to pay their loans. Farming is capital intensive and a risky undertaking, and access credit for farming is already difficult if not impossible. When you add the debt of student loans it is impossible.

Labor is one of the most expensive line item the farmers face every day while farming, next to the capital investments needed to start and maintain a farm. It is very important that the *Teenage Mutant Ninja Turtles* try to do as much as they can by themselves and with family members. It's kind of a double-edged sword, you want to start out small to minimize your costs but you want to be big enough to show a profit and make a living, that's the tricky part. There is a program available for the *Teenage Mutant Ninja Turtles* to take advantage of in regards to a labor source that is (WWOOF) Worldwide Opportunities on Organic Farms, where you can post labor positions and recruit workers to come stay on the farm for room and board plus some cash.

There is one group of labor that is the backbone of the American farmer and the main ally of the *Teenage Mutant Ninja Turtles* and that is the migrant worker. Without them U.S agriculture would crumble. They are the spokes of the American agricultural wheel, and we are in danger of losing them because of the *Slimy-Green Goblin* (Trump) *and his Creatures of the Black Lagoon* (Trump Administration) anti-immigration policies. I don't care if you're a new or old farmer at some point on your farm you will need migrant help, because the "white boys" aren't going to do it. Trust me, I've spent 60 years on farms and no one does better manual labor than the migrant worker. As for the *Slimy-Green Goblin's* infamous Wall, I' dig under it if I have to get my migrant workers for my farm!

Let me ask you something. Whenever you're driving on an inter-state highway, in any state, and you pass a field full of laborers picking a crop, weeding, or moving irrigation lines, take a close look at who's doing the work. Not the white guy in the air-conditioned cab of a $200,000 GPS-guided tractor, but the ones in the hot sun stooped over doing all the hand work. Safe to say it's a migrant worker. You don't see any "white boys" doing it. That's reality folks, (and I'm a white guy with a nineteen year old son and he doesn't like to do it either). As a matter of fact, think about all the crappy non-farming jobs out there, like nurses' aides that clean bed pans in convalescent homes, sewer workers, maids changing all dirty linens, landscapers, ditch diggers, dishwashers etc. This work is mostly done by migrant workers. So next time you're voting to kick these people out of the country just remem-ber who is picking your food and wiping your ass on your death bed. We had better figure out a worker program for the non-documented worker and the "Dreamers" (DACA) Deferred Action for Childhood Arrivals, to keep them as a labor force in the U.S. or we will very soon, be importing all of our food, and flying it over the Wall from Mexico and South America!

DACA is another plan that was created by *Yoda* (Obama) in 2012 to allow the children of immigrants that come to this country to be documented and contribute to our society. They are not permanent residents, and not a citizen. They are documented and receive a work permit. It is a two year program, subject to renewal. DACA basically give the "Dreamers" a path to citizenship. Of course the *Slimy-Green Goblin* and his *Creatures of the Black Lagoon* along with the Grinches have rescinded the DACA agreement. More Dreamers work in the food than any other industry. Sixteen percent of the Dreamers are employed in food preparation and serving alone. There are over 800,000 DACA recipients that live in the U.S.

Dad used a lot of documented and undocumented immigrant workers on the flower farm as I do here on the farm and it never was a problem until we made it a problem. To me it's pretty simple, with all the technology today just develop a green ID card (work visa) like our driver's license they apply to work in the United States for a certain period of time. They get paid a certain wage to be set, they pay in a certain amount of taxes to cover their basic benefits and then they have to return to their homeland. They are allowed to do that for five or ten years. In that period of time there should be a procedure in place that they can apply to become a citizen. They can't become a citizen unless they have this work visa and have worked in this country for at least five years. Hey...that's my start on how to handle the problem. We need the migrant worker in agriculture or we will not survive in this country.

Because of the *Slimy-Green Goblins'* anti-immigration laws Fortune magazine reports that in 2018-2019 farmers are having trouble trying to find enough workers to plant, weed, and harvest crops in California. Vegetable prices are beginning to soar because this shortage of immigrant workers is causing farmers to leave their crops in the fields to rot because they have no workers to pick them. Losses have triggered more than $13 million in just two California counties in early of 2018 according to NBC news. The PEW (The Joseph Newton Pew Foundation) Research Center reports that in 2018 more Mexicans are leaving the U.S. than are coming here. That's not good news for farmers.

Even after facing the challenges of land access, student loan and capital debt and figuring out your labor needs the *Teenage Mutant Ninja Turtles* will have to be entrepreneurs to sell their products. Young farmers surveyed are capitalizing on the demand for local food selling directly to consumers by way of CSA's (Community Supported Agriculture), farmers markets, by growing a wide diversity of crops and livestock.

Eco watch reported that in 2012 local food sales rose to $6.1 billion up from $4.8 in 2008. That's a great trend for the *Teenage Mutant Ninja Turtles*. The 7.8% of the total number of small farms sell direct to the consumer, or to a local distributor. From 2007-2012 there was only a five percent increase in direct marking small farms, whereby in 2002 (17%) and 2007 (32%). There are a number of reasons for this sharp decline. One is with the steady decline in the annual income of small to medium farms, these farms are going out of business after three to seven years, or being bought out by the bigger farms. The *Green-Eyed Monster*(USDA) has substantiated this claim; by reporting that from 2007-2012; a decrease in the value of direct sales, while the larger farms exhibited a greater return through distributors. Eighty percent of the $6.1 billion went through distributors, and on-line sales.

Civil Eats reports that only fifteen percent of retail sales are paid back to the farmers. The rest of the costs are distributed to manufacturing, packaging, transportations, advertising, and marketing, compared to thirty five to forty percent in the 1960-1970's. Basically the *Jolly Green Giant* (Small Farmers) get 25 cents per pound of vegetables and 5 cents for a loaf of bread. Pretty hard for the *Teenage Mutant Ninja Turtles* (Young, millennial farmers) to get excited about those returns!

Marketing the goods for the *Teenage Mutant Ninja Turtles* continues to become a challenge for these up and coming farmers. Over ten years ago there was a huge, "Buy Local" movement; I think it was a fad, because as of 2016 we see a decline in the percentage bought at farmers markets as well as the prices. A lot of these big chains like Walmart and Costco are now bringing in this "fake organic" grown by *Dr. Doom* and its having a detrimental effect on the *Jolly Green Giants' and the Teenage Mutant Ninja Turtles* income. Civil Eats reports that despite the small farmer's commitment to growing sustainable food for their communities, the local communities do not embrace their product enough to keep them in business. This is evident in Quincy, Ca. where the local community has not been able to support small farmers through their restaurants, natural food stores, CSA boxes or farmers markets and five out the seven local farms have closed their doors in the last three years. It's happening all over the country. It's causing the *Jolly Green Giant and the Teenage Mutant Ninja Turtles* to travel long distances to the larger cities to sell their produce. Small farmers are traveling two to three hours one-way to metropolitan cities like Chicago, New York, and San Francisco and it costs them huge amounts of fuel, wear-and-tear on their vehicles, takes them off of the farm and last but not least cuts into an already declining profit.

We are definitely going through some different times, never before seen in America agriculture. Like I said earlier, ten to fifteen years ago there was the "Organic kids" going into farming, they had the dreads, long hair, smoked weed but were passionate about sustainable farming , the survey still shows Millennials are interested in being organic and sustainable, but they seem to be heading toward the corporate model which, in my opinion will be the extinction of the Farmasaur (small family Farm). What made the "organic" and "Buy Local" movement attractive is that It's "what the big stores like Walmart and Costco" cant' give you, which is customer service, and "meet the farmer—know where your food is coming from," that concept is now being replaced by "convenience and price." Let me explain, on-line purchasing have gone through the roof over the past five years. Companies like EBay and Amazon, Blue Apron have mastered the social media and improved technologies well ahead of anything we've ever seen or used before, utilizing app's, robotics, and now cashier-less stores. They have convinced the American public that convenience out values locally fresh. It is very evident in the merger of Amazon buying Whole Foods.

Danielle Beurteaux of Civil Eats says that Whole Foods claims their stores will continue to sell local products and or buyers remain committed to discovering and incubating local and innovative brands. As some "sharp-eyed observers" have noticed, "local" is now hard to find on the website, but "savings" and "new lower prices" are featured. Locating the retailer's local program on line takes a dedicated search or a visit to the site map. While some really worry about the "Amazonification" of Whole Foods could require local producers to compete against the large companies with lower prices—potentially resulting in a dilution of authentic local products (Exactly what's already happening!).

The bigger looming disruption is Amazon's delivery model. Amazon has proven to disrupt markets, and farmers and food producers are worried that they are next. Amazons' delivery model could possibly crush the local retail stores because fewer and fewer people will walk into a local store. That means fewer opportunities for producers to interact and educate the shoppers.

The Washington Post reports that Amazon doesn't have a great tract record of "using the little guy" and farmers and small food producers feel this tech giant will use its market power to further centralize and corporatize its model. This merger will boost and industrialize organic operations to the detriment of small and mid-size players as seen in the "watering down" of organic standards. *Dr. Doom* (Agribusiness) has already pressured the organic community of the NOP and NOSB to cave in on "weakening" the organic standards to allow "fake organic" to infiltrate the big retailers. The merger has already put pressure on reducing prices that will hurt the profits of the mid-sized farmers that they purchase from.

Over the years, before the merger, Whole Foods has increasingly bought from bigger and bigger farms. Ten years ago when Whole Foods moved into Reno, Nevada, they gathered all of us small farmers and gave us a "song and dance" about how they were going to "buy everything we could grow", well I can say after ten years: "they didn't buy anything I grew" As there're corporate model grew so did their regulations that squeezed the small farmer out like high insurance requirements, food safety (GAP requirements), and price setting. Don't be fooled by a "Wolf in sheep's clothing", this merger is disastrous for the *Jolly Green Giant and the Teenage Ninja Turtles.*

CNBC reports that the merger of Amazon and Whole Foods is not only a threat to farmers and small producers but also to restaurants and supermarket retailers. This tech giant has expansive consumer data collection abilities and its on-lie convenience has been a drain on local retailers and restaurants. Supermarkets are a $32 billion industry. Eli Portnoy CEO of Sense 360, and former Amazon employee told CNBC, "right now, most of these items are picked up by consumer's in-stores, but Amazon and its competitor Blue Apron, delivery of fresh-prepared meals can add-a-new level of convenience for consumers. Currently 12% of Americans buy groceries on line in 2016.

This is scary for the incoming millennial farmers because they live their life with app's and techno-devises and the urge for them to jump on board this Amazon bullet train is so tempting, but if you do you are supporting the corporate model and pulling the consumer further away from knowing the farmer and understanding where your food comes from. Not only the organic food can be compromised by these giants but you're adding to the amount of packaging that has to be done for food safety in shipping all these products door to door on a daily basis. We are then contributing to the waste problem in America and the plastic toxic dumps that are happening in our oceans and around the world. We must go back to the farm and buy from the farmer!

Younger generations have been adapting to on-line shopping at a greater pace as they seek convenience over value. Millennials in particular, are leaning toward ordering groceries on line. As the millennials get married and have children they will be buying more groceries on line over the next decade. The direct-to-consumer delivery business is booming, especially in the bigger cities and suburbs and Amazon knows this. AmazonFresh is selling its own brand of meal kits that has crushed Blue Apron since its merger with Whole Foods. Amazon now with having the largest organic retailer in its back pocket can really monopolize the direct-to-consumer delivery model. Since the merger, Blue Apron's stock has plummeted over 44 percent due to the speculation by investors of Amazons impact on the market industry. Millennials please don't fall into this trap!

As a third generation farmers it seems that every generation seems to get further away from understanding where our food comes from, and it's not the fault of the *Teenage Mutant Ninja Turtles,* it's an accumulation over the past two or three generation affected by technology that people are not "getting their hands dirty" anymore. Technology and cheap food has turned Americans into a sedentary (sit at the desk job) life style, looking for convenience over value creating an unhealthy society. The further away you get from "the dirt" the less you understand about where your food comes from.

I look at my generation, coming out of the 1960'-1970's, a large portion of my friends parents were farmers or had a garden in the back yard and we played in the river, rode bikes, threw rocks, and had no kind of electronic devices to entertain us, we entertained ourselves and each other, not like today where kids need to be entertained and stimulated by some sort of electronic device. It was the surge of the first wave of technology. Television was replacing radio, and the white collared- rich people of Hollywood could now be seen as "that's what

I want to be", by all of us kids. Dad would say "Go to college…be somebody, or else you'll be pulling weeds the rest of your life." My friends' parents would tell their daughters to "Go and marry a doctor, lawyer, or a banker…someone with money!" The TV shows depicted the farmer and the blue-collar worker as a "low-life" in a "wife-beater, V-neck t-shirt", all dirty and uneducated like Ralf Cramdon of the Gleason Show who worked in the sewer; the Beverly Hillbillies; Petty Coat Junction…the TV networks even wanted the farmer to look like a white-collar worker in Green Acres. A farmer was someone "you didn't want to be." That negative image has continued through generations and we (farmers) are still fighting that stigma today as one of the least desirable jobs with one of the lowest pay.

Then you moved into the Dot-comers in the 1980's-2000 and it was all about the computer age, Silicon Valley, you weren't just and average white collar worker like an accountant, or retail clerk, teacher, doctor, banker that lived in the suburbs with maybe had a garden; but now you made "mega bucks", living and working in a high rise office or apartment in downtown San Francisco, Chicago, New York and living the "high-life" with no garden or maybe a window-sill planter box with a few herbs in it. The next generation 2000-2008 pretty much followed the same pattern by eating "crappy food", the industrialization of unhealthy foods exploded with McDonald's, Burger King, Wendy's Taco Bell, KFC. Fast food junkies appear during this period eating very little fresh fruits and vegetables, further getting away from "knowing where our food comes from." In this group, most never saw a farm and now only recollect that maybe "grandpa had a garden in the backyard…I don't really remember, I was too young."

It brought us to the group between 2009-2014, the "Organic food, Buy Local" movement, which I call a fad, they are still around but it doesn't seem to have much weight any more, only if it's convenient. These were the "foodies", all the Chef TV shows, Michael Pollan's Omnivores Dilemma, Food Inc. the big food movement to get people off of fast food to eat healthy. Michelle Obama's big organic garden kick off to put organic food into our schools...we were finally on the right track. Maybe now we could get new young farmers to take over for us aging farmers...NOT!!

That brings us to the Millennials, 2015 to the present, a whole new generation of kids. They are the furthest group from the food chain, now pushing three plus generations from a family member ever being a farmer, and very scary. This poses new challenges for this new group of *Teenage Mutant Ninja Turtles* (Young, millennial farmers, which currently make up eight percent of all farmers). They are the highest educated group of farmers that we've ever had to into farming. This high tech breed according to the consumer data collected by CMO.com suggests that millennials own an average of 7.7 internet devices and use 3.3 of them daily. The American Farm bureau suggest that these group of upcoming farmers are adept to using agro-technology, GPS-self-driven tractors, hyper-weather equipment apps, precision farming sensors and real time analysis along with new drone technology. Just what *Dr. Doom* (Agribusiness) is looking for! He must be licking his chops right now, drooling over this new class of farmers that he can manipulate and brainwash and develop their GMO franken-foods and operate their drones and GPS driven tractors and harvesters. It is us older farmers that must play *YODA* (Mentors) and steer these new farmers in the right direction toward the pure ways of organic, sustainable farming.Folks this is not good for the *Jolly Green Giant and the Teenage Ninja Turtles*. You can see the pattern here, not only will the *Teenage Ninja Turtles* have to contend with *Dr. Dooms'* mega farms but now we see the consolidation of *Dr. Dooms'* agrifoods conglomerate WholeFoods/Amazon that not only will be pushing mid-size farmers to get bigger, but they are becoming more successful in convincing the consumer that "convenience outweighs value." If this mentality continues the small to mid-size farmers are definitely done. Once you take away the one-on-one concept of "meet your farmer—see where your food comes from, it will be the end of the *Jolly Green Giant and the Teenage Mutant Ninja Turtles,* because that's all we have to hang on to is our local farmers markets, CSA boxes, local chef's restaurants and a few natural food stores. As a small farmer, the more I see where the direction is going (which is away from small farms) I feel for the *Teenage Mutant Ninja Turtles...*"The noose is getting tighter and I feel my boot starting to slip off the chair." We must have a New Green Deal that redirects to focus of American agriculture back to the small farmer to grow local and regional food and food products to support our local communities again and bring back the "mom and pop" local businesses to keep our money supporting our local communities and creating local jobs.

Mayonnaise, like hollandaise was invented by the French to cover up the flavor of spoiled flesh, stale vegetables, rotten fish. Beware the Sauce! Where food comes beslobbered with an elegant slime you may well suspect the integrity of the basic ingredient.--Edward Abbey

Green Light

Grow Green

"The future will be green or not at all"

Bob Brown

The color of green relates to harmony and balance. It renews and restores depleted energy. It is the guiding light for new, young farmers to replace us aging farmers and look at new creative ways to sustain small farms in the future. Being a combination of yellow and blue, green is made up of the optimism of yellow with the calmness and insight of blue, inspiring hope (for young farmers) and generosity of spirit not available from other colors which epitomize the young and incoming small farmer.

It will be the responsibility of us older farmers during our Golden years to mentor this group of young and upcoming men and women farmers (millennials) to take over our farms. It is a daunting task, but I believe in the next generation of upcoming farmers. These young farmers will have more than Twenty-Seven Shades of Green to face in the upcoming years and must be up to the task. The Point reports that 82% of the millennials are favorable for flexible schedules, working at home, and value experiences over material goods which help loving what they like to do—Farming.

The next generation of farmers is coming from the cities, ditching the suits and grabbing the pitchforks! Millennials are far more likely than the general farming population to grow organically, limit pesticide and fertilizer use, diversify their crops and animals, and be involved in their local community food systems The millennials tend to operate small farms of less than 50 acres and women constitute thirty percent of all farmers, with fourteen percent being primary operators, with 91%, of female-operated farms having less than $50,000 in sales.

Going into the future we must "Grow Green" in our culture, giving the "Green light" to our new generation of farmers to take over. We must be more creative than we've ever been for small farmers to survive. The odds are stacked against them, between 1992- 2012 the Washington Post reports that the country has lost 250,000 small-mid-size farms and has an increase of 35,000 mega farms, and that's not a good indicator for the beginning farmer. The number of young farmers entering the field is nowhere enough to replace the existing, aging farmer. A staggering statistic is that from 2007-2012 agriculture gained 2,384 new farmers between the ages of 25-34, but lost 100,000 farmers between the ages of 45-54 because they can't sustain their farms. I hate to see the 2016 census the trend has been getting worse.

So what can we do for the young incoming farmers? According to the National Young Farmers Coalition (NYFC), they have proposed a Young Farmers Agenda to the USDA and Congress for suggestions to the 2018 Farm Bill. Despite President Trump's threat to gut the Farm Bill by 21% they are pleading their case to help new beginning farmers. The 2014 Farm Bill helped create additional on-ramps for new producers, but despite the millions that went into training and supports for new programs young farmers, USDA didn't put their money where the problems continue and that's for land access, available low interest loans and credit to reduce farmer debt and a guest worker program that works for farmers. That all has to be reversed and reversed quickly.

The NYFC reports that forty percent of the young farmers trying to use the USDA 2014 Farm Bill programs said that the applications and the paperwork were too cumbersome and burdensome and not applicable to helping the farmer, Some thirty percent were unfamiliar with the programs and the USDA staff had no clue what the programs even were, and twenty eight percent said the local USDA staff were too hard to work with and the process took way too long.

These are the same reoccurring problems that happen with the Farm bill programs as I allotted to in my 2013 book: *Why I Farm: Risking it all for a Life on the Land,* the program applications are too cumbersome, too long, take way too much time to fill out and most are for training, and conservation programs, and none for land purchase, or accessible farm credit. Most are pretty much worthless to the new and newly established farmers.

Some proposals in the Young Farmers Agenda are to:

- Hire training agents to work with young farmers to get them through the process.
- To update USDA services to put all the applications on line and develop "easy-to-use" apps, and streamline the process.
- To create a "micro" loan process that's easy and fast to remove the burdensome paperwork.
- To improve the Agriculture Conservation Easement Program to improve the process to purchase easements on farmland.
- To increase the match from 50% to 75% for farmers.
- In 2013 the NYFC reported that 25% of the agricultural land trusts have seen these lands sit vacant with no farmers working the land. These lands must become available to farmers.
- To increase funding for the Farm Service Agency (FSA) Create more available low interest loans and lines of credit for small farmers and increase the loan amount for land purchase from $300,000 to at least $500,000. Farm land real estate values have increased by 40% or more since 2008.
- Create loan forgiveness, repayment or refinance program for all small farmers to pay off or forgive student loan debt and allow

refinancing of high interest loans of farmers.

- Establish a tax-free savings account for farmers to have access to credit lines and for risk managements assessments and to lower farm insurance costs, and access to affordable health care.
- To improve programs for farmer training in technology, agriculture, trades, conservation, and marketing of their goods.

The Young Farmers Agenda that has been proposed to Congress and the USDA has many hopes and aspirations for young farmers. I suppose you could say that "It can only get better", but the reality is "it's not" with the direction of this Administration and USDA who have blatantly admitted that their priority is to help the large, mega farms. I hope they throw a "few pennies" at the problem but we have to have another plan.

I have faith that the young farmers (millennials) will be resilient and rise to the challenges that face the future of farming. Some of the "Geek Squad" will be recruited to help the agribusiness, corporate-mega farms to operate the new age of robotics, drones, GPS-self-driven tractors and the technologies of GMO foods, and bio-chemistry pesticides etc. But I hope the majority will find a way to go back to the land like their forefathers and mentors.

The survival of the small farmer is also in part, in the hands of the consumers. In quoting Michael Pollan, "people have to vote with their fork." There will be no financial incentives for fruits and vegetable growers and we will be at odds against the "Amazonification" of the food industry. The consumer must "attack the Brand" of the McDonalds, Whole Foods, Walmart, Costco and hit them where it hurts and that's on image to the public. The government, lobbyists, and politicians are in the back pockets of these corporate giants, and they have the money, but if you can tarnish their "image" to the American public they will buckle. As seen by sexual harassment claims and by abusing immigrant worker conditions and pay. "Boycott the Brand" as

Michael Pollen quoted in Robert Reich's Interview: *The Achilles Heel of American Capitalism*. The bottom line is that the consumer holds the reins. They need to pull back on these reins and turn this stage-coach back to the land and bring back local food to our communities and embellish our local businesses and put money back into our local economies and not in the pockets of these corporate giants.

The consumer has to avoid the Costco's and Walmart's and go back to getting their CSA boxes (Community Supported Agriculture), go to their weekly farmers markets and buying from roadside stands. They have to avoid the temptation of convenience. Get off your lazy ass and patronize your local farmers and buy healthy wholesome foods that are nutritious and locally made or grown and not all that processed fast food in the middle isles of the supermarket. Help reduce the epidemics of obesity, cancer, heart disease and diabetes. In the meantime while you're doing that get some exercise by walking to the market or better yet volunteer at your local community garden to pull some weeds, help at your local farm or even grow your own garden… how novel is that!!.

For you small and young farmers, my advice is to put your lap tops, and electronic devices on the kitchen table until night time. Get out on the land and "stay there", it's time for what I call the "Coffee-can Revolution", where "cash is king", and barter is everything. It's all about the "Green-Stuff"! That's how Nonno made it, Dad made it… and I've made it, still today. Put 100% of your effort on direct sales to consumers for cash. Stash that cash, every penny for that piece of used equipment you need on Craig's' list, seed, or for the off-season to pay your rent. Over the years I've chipped away at loans, building my cash markets here on the farm in any way I could farmers markets, plant sales, pumpkin patches, barn dinners, tours, concerts, and "go fund me projects".

Don't look at your "How much did I make an hour, or the college formula of "pay yourself a wage", you can't, its irrelative when you start out, so just deal with it." It's a lifestyle, and that's what you signed up to do, you'll have to work 70-80 hour weeks for the first three to five years before you figure it out, and you'll have to give up the "millennial corporate-'high price gadgets" because it's all about "garage sale shovels and pitchforks." The key to success is to diverse your operation with high dollar crops, niche markets and getting the top dollar by selling direct to the consumer as much as possible and promoting your farm and label is the key. Don't sell yourselves short, especially if you grow organically and sustainably your products are at the utmost value to the consumer. You are the Farmasaurs. You are the "Jurassic Farmer" that everyone wants to come and see! Build on it, the locals want to meet the farmer, so at night when you come in, pick up your cell phone go out take pictures of that day, that praying mantis "munching a bug on your sunflowers" or your eight your old daughter all dirty carrying an armful of bunched carrots, and post it on social media… that's what you millennials were born to do!

Create farm stands on your farm, and agritourism events, get creative and get people to the farm!!! Do like we did recruiting 10-20 local farmers, crafters, and food vendors to set up a farmers market on your farms, and have them pay you for stall fees. Why are you paying some other guy who could care less about the farmers, who just wants to "fill spots" to keep the "green-stuff" that should be in your pocket, and sticks you on some hot pavement in an abandoned parking lot?

People will tell you that "oh…farmers markets take you off the farm and that hampers the production of the farm. Well let me tell you this with a family of four we have been able to keep five to ten acres in full production every week, year round, attending three to five markets a week for three generations since 1921 and nobody can sell their own goods better than the farmer him/herself! These farm bill, government projects did absolutely nothing for me, nor did I ever depend on them, and I never qualified for any of the programs. Until I see one small farmer rely on one of these programs I'll continue burying my "coffee-can "in the back yard, and create my own legacy.

I think in reality, in the next 20 years, most of our fresh fruits and vegetables in American will come from Mexico and South America. I've done some extensive research using CCOF's (California Certified Organic Farmers) membership data and only a handful of small farmers will be speckled around our local communities because if agribusiness continues to lose migrant workers at its current pace, they will move their operations to Mexico and South America where labor is cheap and export is nearby.

We are becoming a food desert in America. The U.S. has some of the richest soil in the world with the best knowledge in technology and agriculture and the wealthiest nation on earth, but we are the most unhealthy people of all the industrial nations, but annually we are importing more food, especially fruits and vegetables to America than we are exporting.

According to statistics from CCOF:

- 2014 there were only 45 certified organic farms in Mexico
- 2017 there were 133 organic farms in Mexico
- 2018 it grew substantially to 195 organic farms in Mexico encompassing almost 80,000 organic acres
- Mexico is growing about 50% of the U.S. supply of berries, mango's, avocados
- Mexico is growing 25% of America's supply of mixed vegetables, tomatoes, citrus and greens, and processed foods

That's a 32% increase in organic farms within one year (2017-2018), and over three times the amount since 2014. So why the sudden increase in organic farms opening up in Mexico? Well it's pretty simple. If you look at the crops predominantly being raised in Mexico it's the ones that are the most labor intensive, that have to be hand-picked such as berries, mixed vegetables, tree-fruits, tomatoes, and greens. Because of the anti-immigration policies here in America, large agribusiness companies are moving their operations to Mexico and South American where the labor is cheap. As I noted earlier, that's why more Mexicans are moving back to Mexico than coming to the United States. We are creating our Food Desert.

Not only is the labor so cheap, but the paper trail of keeping a certified organic product "legitimate" all the way to your kitchen table is diminished, because through export channels there are more ways "fake organic" products can be switched out or contaminated along the transport channels. Once the farms are inspected for organic certification, there is no way to make sure that that organic avocado leaves as "organic" and arrives at your table as "organic." This will become a major problem the more that agribusiness controls our food supply, especially coming from a foreign country. In the future this will cause more food safety issues and major recalls of hundreds of products because the further a product travels without control the higher the chance of contamination that can occur.

Please note that this research that I have done is only for CCOF certified farms which only accounts for maybe 40% of all organic certified farms. There are a number of other third-party organic certifiers that are not included in my research, and all of the conventional (non-organic) farms are not included at all. If you look at the big picture of food produced in the U.S. in general, most foods are being imported to the U. S. It's staggering to see that we don't export much at all other than corn, grains, rice, soybean, and cotton, which are mostly GMO crops. So in a sense all we are doing is polluting the world and ourselves with GMO processed foods and these crops. Pretty sad.

USDA reports that Mexico is the most important supplier of fresh produce to the U.S. accounting for 70% of the U.S. fresh vegetable in 2016, up from an import value of 40% in 2014. In 2012 Mexico accounted for $4.05 billion in fruit imports to the U.S. and with three times the amount of farms moving to Mexico since then the reports must be to a staggering $10 plus billion. USDA reports that our imports from Mexico for fruits and vegetables have raised an average of twenty percent per year. There is no way Mexico will ever pay for the Wall that President Trump wants because the U.S. Goods and trade deficit with Mexico is over $63.2 billion as of 2017. We currently import more goods from Mexico ($294.2 Billion) than we export to Mexico ($231 billion).

As for South American countries, Chile is our biggest importer of tropical and tree fruits totaling over $5 billion in 2017, and increasing imports an average of ten percent per year. Peru is second in fruits and vegetables providing about 5 percent of the U.S. supply and has grown 31 percent in imports to the U.S. since 1999.

According to the U.S. Department of Commerce since 2015 U.S. exports declined to the lowest levels since 2010 and our imports continually rose an average of two percent per year.

Our main export crops are:

- Tree nuts (walnuts, almonds, pistachio) which account for 70% of all U.S. produced.
- Cotton and wheat account for 50% of U.S. produced.
- Pork and processed foods account for 15% of all produced.

Our top imports and importers are:

- Over 44% of U.S. imports are horticultural products such as fruits, vegetables, tree nuts, essential oils, nursery stock, cut flowers and hops.
- An additional 25% imports are tropical crops, sugar, coffee, cocoa, and rubber tropical crops.
- In general, imports of vegetable oils (GMO), processed grain products, red meat, and dairy have grown significantly in recent years.
- In organic foods our top imports are bananas, coffee, olive oil, and corn & soybean (because we can't grow organic corn or soybean in the U.S. anymore because 99% is GMO).
- Our top importers of organic products are: Turkey, Mexico,

Italy, Peru, Chile, and Ecuador, which imports 45% of tracked organic products to the U.S.

- In all, over 87 countries supply organic products to the U.S.

So to feed the American unhealthy diet, we import:

- 95% of our coffee, cocoa, and spices
- 90% of our fish and shellfish
- 50% or more of our fresh fruits and berries
- 35% of our sugar, wine, vegetable oil
- Over 25% of our fresh vegetables and processed foods.

As we grow less food in this country and import more food from foreign countries we will get more generations away from understanding where our food comes from and with the advances of technology that promotes "convenience over quality of life (value)" we will become a national food desert.

These import and export statistics proves my theory right that both conventional and organic farms are moving their operations to Mexico and other foreign countries to grow our fruits and vegetables and as we import more food because of a variety of reasons i.e. labor costs, operational costs, lower land values, year round operation etc. In the incoming years we will see more of our food outsourced to be grown in these foreign countries by our U.S. mega farms and agribusinesses that will relocate to these countries and reap the farm bill subsides to do so and the tax credits. In my estimation, within twenty years the only agriculture that will exist is the large industrial farms growing mechanized crops like wheat, rice, soybean, corn, cotton that do not require hand labor. All hand labor intensive,(hand-weeding, hand-harvest, hand sorting, hand packing hand-picked, etc.) crops will be out sourced to farms in Mexico and south American countries and imported to the U.S. The agribusiness mega food corporations will follow the corporate model of the other overseas industries (computer, industrial, banking) to grow our food.

In closing, I don't think we are going to change the thinking of the "masses", that the trend is going towards "convenience over value" and small farmers have to realize that we're dependent on the advances of technology whether we like it or not, "folks...people want to sit at home and use an app on their cell phone and have fresh "so-called" organic vegetables delivered to their table by Amazon along with all their other goods"...and us small farmers can't compete with that pricing. Those organic and conventional foods are going to come from somewhere other than the U.S. Us small farmers will be the "Mad Max" characters trying to survive in an evil world of "Frankenstein foods" in an unhealthy environment.

For us small farmers we must again strive to build healthy local communities to reach out and keep that 5-10% of the population that still want to support local farmers by buying their fresh organic produce at farmers markets, CSA programs, farm stands, local natural food stores, and food hubs.

We really need to look at the shades of green that surrounds and influences the farm, from the money of green; to the fields of green; to our feelings of green; and the dark sides of green; and continue this way of life, love of the land to "Grow- Green" for our families, neighbors, and local communities. We all need to strive to be better human beings to our fellow man and our environments. It is the small farmer again, despite all the advanced technology that is the ultimate steward of the land that works with the ominous forces of Mother Nature that are changing our climate (climate change) to grow our food, organically, and sustainably to nourish our local food sheds and help protect our air, land, and water.

In the end, our children will still be farming our twenty-seven shades of green and many more after it's all said and done. The aging farmers will continue to mentor our future farmers of all ages and growing all shades of green will continue to be the true colors of the small American farmer.

We have neglected the truth that a good farmer is a craftsman of the highest order, a kind of artist...People need to feed themselves, next they need to feed their communities.

Wendell Berry

Gary Romano outstanding in my field.

www.ingramcontent.com/pod-product-compliance
Lightning Source LLC
Chambersburg PA
CBHW031434270326
41930CB00007B/702